W OF
ILLE
A,

CHURCH

BAY OF QUINTE

ALBERT COLLEGE.

MANUFACTORIES:

Nº 22. J.M. WALKER & CO. .. FOUNDRY & MACHINE S.
23. J. & G. BROWN
24. E. BURRELL..AX. FACTORY.
25. IRVIN DIAMOND-FLOURING MILL.
26. A.N. PRINGLE.. PLANING MILL. SASH DOOR
27. W.H. VERMILYEA .. CARRIAGE FACTORY.
28. FLINT & HOLTON..STEAM SAW & PLANING
29. RATHBURN & SON . STEAM MILL & LUMBER
30. WOOLEN. MILLS.
31. VICTORIA.. FOUNDRY.
32. PLANING MILLS.
33. ELEVATORS.

EY, PROPRIETOR.
SE. G. HOGGARD, PROP.
OTEL..T.A. HOLBROOK.

ON
A HOUSE.
WAY
ER HOTELS.

Second Edition

To commemorate the Centennial
of the City of Belleville

Coat of Arms of the City of Belleville

HISTORIC BELLEVILLE

by
Nick and Helma Mika

Mika Publishing Company
Belleville, Ontario
1977

Historic Belleville
Copyright © Mika Publishing Company, 1977
ISBN 0-919303-16-1
FC3099.B44M54   971.3'585   C77-001396-1
F1059.5   B44M54
Printed and bound in Canada
Paper: Lustro Offset Enamel Dull Cream 200M
Type: Baskerville
Printed by The Intelligencer, Belleville, Ontario

NOTICE.

APPLICATION will be made by the Council of the Corporation of the Town of Belleville to the next sitting of the Legislature of the Province of Ontario, for one or more Acts as may be necessary to incorporate the Town of Belleville as a City, to be called the " CITY OF BELLEVILLE," and also to consolidate the debt of the said Town or City, and to enable the Council thereof to issue new Debentures for the payment of the existing debt, as the same matures or otherwise, and for other purposes connected therewith,

Dated this 20th day of November, A. D. 1876.

By order of the Town Council,
R. NEWBERY,
Clerk of the Municipality of
the Town of Belleville.
1t aw-6w.

GRAND
Celebration !

Inauguration of the

CITY of BELLEVILLE

—ON—

Dominion Day, 1878,

The inauguration will commence with a

Grand Procession,

Consisting of Military (the 15th and 49th Battalions,) about 500 Firemen, with their respective Bands, also the Tradesmen of the City, representing the different branches of industry in full operation, and the Citizens in carriages. The procession to form at the City Hall at 10 o'clock in the morning, and headed by the Military and Oddfellows Bands, will proceed through the principal streets of the City to the

Agricultural Grounds

$500 ALL CASH PRIZES.

At the hour of one o'clock, the following Programme of Athletic Sports and Caledonian Games will be proceeded with under the able management of Chief Hugh McKinnon who won the Great Athletic Championship at the International contest in Philadelphia, in 1876. In these games the most noted Athletes on the Continent will take part. Open to all comers.

List of Games and Prizes Offered for Competition.

	DESCRIPTION OF GAMES	1st.	2d.	3d
1	Putting the Heavy Stone, 21 lbs.	$10	$5	$2
2	Putting the Light Stone, 14 lbs.	10	5	2
3	Standing Jump,	10	5	2
4	Reel of Tulloch, in Highland Costume	10	5	2
5	Short Race, 100 yards,	10	5	2
6	Vaulting with pole,	10	5	2
7	Running Jump,	10	5	2
8	Running Hop Step and Jump,	10	5	2
9	Broad Sword Dancing, in Higland Costume,	10	5	2
10	Standing High Jump,	10	5	2
11	Running High Jump,	10	5	2
12	Bagpipe playing Strathspey and Reel,	10	5	2
13	Hurdle Race, 200 yards,	10	5	2
14	Hitch and Kick,	10	5	2
15	One Mile Race,	15	5	2
16	Best Dressed Highlander,	10	5	2
17	Walking Match, one Mile	10	5	2
18	Highland Fling, in Costume,	10	5	2
19	Throwing the Heavy Hammer,	10	5	2
20	Throwing the Light Hammer	10	5	2
21	Race, 440 yards	10	5	2
22	Tossing the Caber,	10	5	2
23	Bagpipe Playing Pibroch and March,	10	5	2
24	Threesome Reel, (3 Hand Reel,)	10	5	2
25	Sack Race,	10	5	2
26	Quoits, outside the Ring,	10	5	2
27	Boys' Race, 14 years and under 150 yards,	5	3	2

REGULATIONS:—1. The Rules of the North American United Caledonian Association will govern all games and competitions. 1. No person allowed inside the Ring except competitors members of the press, and judges. 3. Competitors will make their entries with the Secretary on the grounds ; Four Entries in each game or no competition. 4. Last Entry to lead off. 5. An entrance fee of 25 cents will be charged for each game.

Torch Light Procession !

A Grand Torch Light Procession of the Firemen will take place from the City Hall, at the hour of 8 o'clock, proceeding through the different streets of the City, thence to the Agricultural Grounds, where Prof. Hand, from Hamilton, will proceed with his Brilliant

DISPLAY OF FIREWORKS

He is considered to be the best Pyrotechnic Artist in the Dominion.

— —

A Civic Banquet

will take place at 6 o'clock, p. m.

Refreshments may be procured on the Grounds from 12 o'clock to 3 p. m. Special arrangements have been made with the G. T. Railway for Single Fare east and west for that day, and Steamboats at Excursion rates. Entrance to Grounds 25cts.; Children 10cts. Entrance to Grounds, Fireworks, 15 cts.; Children 10cts.

A. EX. ROBERTSON,
Mayo .

D. B. ROBERTSON,   MORGAN JELLETT,   Hon. Secretary.
Hon. Treasurer.

Alex Robertson
Mayor of Belleville

About three o'clock on the morning of Sunday July 1, 1878, Bellevillians were awakened by the booming of a cannon.

As the morning dawned, still and very hot, the streets of the city began to come alive. Country people started to arrive on horseback, in buggies, on lumber wagons, carts, and on foot. Some had driven all night in order to be on hand early and find accommodations for themselves and their horses. By eight o'clock in the morning streets were thronged with people and vehicles. Hotels and livery stables were filled to capacity. Hundreds more arrived throughout the early morning hours by excursion steamers from Watertown across Lake Ontario, from Trenton, Picton, Napanee and Kingston.

The crowd was in a jubilant mood. Relatives, friends and strangers had come to help Bellevillians celebrate the birthday of their city. And celebrate they did in a manner befitting the important occasion, with parades, speeches, games, banquets and fireworks.

Officially Belleville had become a city on December 31, 1877, but festivities to mark the event had been postponed to coincide with Dominion Day 1878.

Shortly before the great day, the *Daily Ontario*, one of the city's two newspapers, had appealed to its readers:

Hang your banners on the outer walls and
let signs and symbols speak the sentiments
of your hearts. Wherever a flag can be thrown
to the breeze, there let the national emblem flutter . . .

Citizens of Belleville spared neither efforts nor expense to show their pride in their city. Front Street was a sight to behold with its magnificent and richly embellished evergreen arches, festoons, flags and streamers. Businesses and private homes were gaily decorated, and at night streets and homes were illuminated with candles and Chinese lanterns.

According to the *Intelligencer* of July 2, 1878, this is how Bellevillians and their visitors celebrated the once-in-a-lifetime occasion:

Daily Intelligencer.

BELLEVILLE, TUESDAY, JULY 2.

THE CITY OF BELLEVILLE.

Grand Inaugural Celebration.

THE DEMONSTRATION A COMPLETE SUCCESS.

Splendid Decorations — Gorgeous Procession—Brilliant Illuminations—Magnificent Display of Fireworks.

25,000 Strangers in Town.

BELLEVILLE AT ITS BEST.

FULL ACCOUNT OF THE PROCEEDINGS.

The inaugural day of any city of recent birth has been observed in a manner which went to show that its inhabitants took a just pride in the event, and there is no reason why it should not be so observed, especially as it is the most important occurrence in the history of any place. With its becoming a city the Corporation itself assumes many changes and alterations. Town Councillors are unheard of, as their cognomen becomes Alderman. The Town Clerk becomes the City Clerk, the Town Constable becomes an officer, and other changes occur which take off the flavor of everything town-like and gives it a metropolitan spice. The Mayor also becomes a more prominent official than he formerly was, his office generally (the act is permissive) calls for a salary, he is provided with robes of state, and though he may be annoyed with the many and frequent calls made upon him, it is safe to assume as in all human affairs that he enjoys the sweets and comforts of his berth, and enjoys his *otium come dignitate* in a manner worthy of the high position the people have seen fit to place him in. The statutes also provide for other conveniences, which in time we may doubtless take advantage of, and it is to be hoped when we do, the result will prove beneficial for us. When Brantford and St. Catharines became cities their inaugural day was celebrated in an appropriate manner. Particularly so was that of the latter, when a celebration magnificent in its proportions and grand in its character, took place. It was the general desire here that our inaugural should be worthy of the City of the Bay and creditable to all who took part in it. True, Belleville became a city on the 31st of December last, but as the weather at that time of the year is altogether unfitted for the holding of an out-door demonstration, it was deemed advisable to postpone the event to a future day. Dominion day was eventually decided on and arrangements made accordingly. A programme of events was arranged; it was varied and attractive in its character, pleasing in its proportions and generally acceptable in detail. The coming of the day was anxiously looked forward to, and efforts were made on every hand to make it a prominent as well as a successful and attractive event. A trade procession was devised, games were instituted in which athletes could show their energies; visitors and strangers were asked to aid us, and their response was certainly a fitting one. From early morn, the various thoroughfares leading to the city were alive with waggon loads of human freight, and such was the extent of the influx of strangers, that hotel accommodation was insufficient, for the time being, for the purpose, and all the available yard room in the city, and the stables as well, were filled to repletion. And every steamer that came added to the list, so that when the middle of the forenoon had been reached, our principal thoroughfares were thronged with a dense mass of men, women and children, estimated at not less than 25,000, all being eager and anxious for the sights, and if one were to judge from appearances, they were well pleased with the effect. Expressions of admiration were elicited by the holiday appearance of our City. The arches were most admired, whilst the decorations of the buildings on the line of march called forth remarks of general approval, and the weather was fine, though very hot. The procession in the morning was simply grand. The features of the afternoon were quite attractive, whilst the night display excelled anything hitherto attempted. As a whole the celebration was grandly successful, and all who took part in it are to be congratulated on the success of their endeavours to make the display exceed anything yet attempted in this locality. Below will be found a full report of the events of the day.

THE ARRIVALS

At about 6 o'clock in the morning the *Kincardine* arrived with the Watertown Fire Coys. Nos. 1 and 2, with the band of the 35th

Batt. and excursionists altogether to the number of about 125. Although they arrived earlier than expected, they were met by a number of the members of the Fire Brigade, with the Oddfellows' band, who saluted the arriving guests with "Yankee Doodle", beautifully played, upon which performances the Watertown men complimented them very highly. They were escorted to the rooms of No. 1 Fire Company, whose guests they were.

Messrs. A. M. Knickerbocker, City Editor of the *Morning Dispatch,* and Mr. Chaffey, also of the Watertown press, and Aldermen J. E. Bergin and Thos. Barber, arrived with the party.

At about the same hour Hose Coy. No. 2 of Cobourg arrived by train, having with them the Fountain Hose Band. They brought with them a very beautiful Hose cart. They were met at the station by Captain Cummins and a number of the members of Hose Company No. 2, whose guests they were.

The steamer *Utica,* arrived at half-past seven from Trenton having on board about 200 — followed by the *Alexandra* from the same place with 135 and the *Annie Gilbert* with about 40 excursionists.

At 10 o'clock the *City of Belleville* arrived from Picton with 250 passengers, between that and noon the *Pierrepont* arrived from Napanee with 500 excursionists, the *Armenia* from Picton with about the same number, and the *Shannon* from Napanee with about 100 more.

THE DECORATIONS

The nature and extent of the decorations far surpassed anything ever seen here before, and formed the theme of universal admiration. Grand as was the appearance of Belleville on the occasion of the Prince of Wales' visit, it was far — very far — surpassed on the present occasion. It is of course a matter of impossibility to describe all the decorations, but herewith we give a very full description of

Steamer Alexandria.

Steamer Alexandria

the most noteworthy of the displays made on the route of the procession.

Front Street and City Hall

Immediately in front of the business establishment of H. Corby & Sons, and extending across the street to the Queen's Hotel, a very handsome arch was erected. The height of the pillars was 20 feet and from the ground to the centre of the arch underneath, 28 feet. In the manner of decoration it was both unique and attractive. The arch was surmounted with liquor barrels, on the greater number of which were the names of brands of whiskies manufactured by this firm. On the summit three large barrels were placed; the topmost one bore the inscription, "1829, H. Corby & Sons, Millers, Distillers and Wine Merchants," whilst on the heads of two immediately beneath it were the cordial mottoes "Prosperity to our City" and

"Friends, we Greet You." The pillars, which were neatly covered with evergreens, were each surmounted with a puncheon ornamented with small flags. Two Union Jacks floated from flagstaffs near the summit of the arch and stringers of the national ensign as well as lines of bunting, added largely to the general appearance of the structure. At the bases of the arch a wide line of evergreens extended to the Queen's Hotel and Corby & Son's store, and on them were the mottoes "Canada our Home," "Support Home Manufacturers," "Success to our Dominion," and "Welcome to our Guests." From the corners of the pillars festoons extended across the street to the opposite buildings, and from a rope stretched across the street above the arch were suspended the Union Jack and Stars and Stripes. The novelty of this arch, aside from the manner of its decoration, drew a great deal of attention to it, and a large meed of praise was accorded those to whose generosity and liberality its construction was due. From this point to Dundas Street the ornamentation was not of a profuse character, yet the decorations of the Prince Edward and Commercial Hotels, and that in front of the Hon. Lewis Wallbridge's, added much to the appearance of the locality. On Dundas Street the exhibit is limited to displays of small "Jacks." On Church Street, and about midway between Dundas and Bridge Streets, Mr. J. T. Lattimer and the residents of that vicinity had constructed an arch, the pillars of which were 20 feet high, and the centre 29 feet. It was covered with evergreens, and was handsomely set off with flags, bunting and wreaths. The mottoes on this arch were "Our Guests," and "The Land we left and the Land we live in." This arch, although late in being constructed, was very neat and creditable.

Between Mr. Lattimer's residence and the terrace was a small arch, whilst the front of the latter was nicely ornamented with wreaths and green trees. Over the gates in front of Mr. John Robertson's a neat little arch was built, as was also one at Ald. McIninch's, who also made a number of decorations, as did Mr. James Mackie, at his residence. Mr. J. P. Reeves' residence was one of the most tastefully decorated of any of the houses on the line of procession. The verandah and windows were festooned with evergreens, decorated with garlands of flowers, whilst depending from the verandah were a crown of parti-colors, a heart enclosed in a circlet the former bearing the word "Welcome," and a wreath of evergreens, the whole finished with small flags and presenting an extremely neat appearance. The first arch on the line of march on Bridge Street is a small one at the Rectory gate; similar ornaments are also noticeable at Mrs. Furnival's and Mr. James Nosworthy's. On Charles street and opposite the residence of Mr. John J. B. Flint a very large British ensign was strung across the street. Some of the residences on this street were appropriately decorated and presented a very cheerful aspect.

From Charles, down Hotel to Pinnacle and along that to Great St. James, there was little pretence towards display or ornament except Mr. Conger's, and Mr. J. J. B. Flint's, who made a neat exhibit.

The space occupied by Brown's Foundry and Machine Shops was very nicely decorated. Evergreens were placed around the entire block, whilst a platform within and level with the top of the high fence on the Mill Street side did duty for the display of a number of horse rakes gaily decorated. At the south end of the sales room a neat grotto was constructed. It was provided with two floors, on which were placed a variety of agricultural implements. The grotto was ornamented with a number of flags on the sides, whilst the "lion and unicorn" aided in decorating the end. The tenement house opposite this gave ample evidence of the taste of its inmates in the character of its decorative display. As the business portion of the city was reached "decorations" appeared to be the order of the day. Hodge's grocery and Snell's butcher store were well set off, as was also Doyle's Hotel and Moore's Marble Shop and Yard. The exterior of the Masonic Buildings gave every evidence of a desire to aid in honoring the day, as in addition to the abundance of evergreens thereabouts, flags innumerable gave the necessary relief for an advantageous display. On the windows of the hall of the Irish Catholic Benevolent Union were the initial letters of the name of the Society. A harp in green was agreeably conspicuous as a reminder of the nationality of the members, whilst the flag of the Society and a Union Jack hung from each window of their hall. Independent Hose Company No. 2, seemed to manifest an especial pride in the display at their hall and therefore it is almost needless to add the decorations there were of an attractive order. In front of Mr. W. Y. Mikel's, that gentleman assisted by several friends built an arch extending across the street to Fitzpatrick's. The pillars of this were 30 feet high, and from each a line of evergreens ran to the opposite buildings; it was supplied with flag poles at the ends and centre and was handsomely decked with bunting and rosettes, whilst the following mottoes were conspicuous thereon; "Success to our city" and "Prosperity to the Workingmen" and underneath "Erected by W. Y. Mikel and friends," J. N. Redick, builder. All the stores in this locality were nicely decorated and ornamented and looked very neat. The front of the building occupied by Mr. R. Elvins and the Ontario House and the stores of Dr. Dorland and J. Ivers & Co. presented a very cheerful appearance, decked as they were in wreaths of green and otherwise ornamented, whilst Graham's block on the opposite side was no less spicy in its style of display. The show of trimmed pine, spruce and cedar extended onward on the east side, the principal exhibits being that at the Willard House and R. Toy's store, which latter was attired in a very neat garb, as was also the building immediately to the south. On the lot in front of J. M. Walker & Co's foundry that firm erected a stand which was provided with seats from which their friends obtained an excellent view of the procession as it passed along. The stand looked bright and enticing, whilst the character of its decorations reflected credit on those who performed the work. Large and small Union Jacks waved from it on all sides. This firm showed here some of the implements manufactured by them, the display being quite attractive. The motto "Union is Strength" adorned the top of the front of the structure, whilst underneath was a painting with a representation thereon of the industrious beaver and also the figure of an axe. The display at the Albion Hotel showed to excellent advantage. At the livery building of Mr. Lawrence O'Brien that gentleman made quite a prominent and novel show. In addition to the front of the establishment being well decorated a platform was erected and handsomely trimmed, and on it was the figure of a horse in harness hitched to a trotting wagon. This was an attraction of an excellent order, and merited the commendations bestowed upon it. Brown & St. Charles' carriage factory, Davis' harness shop and O'Brien's Hotel shone forth to excellent advantage in their attire of festoons and other devices in evergreens, whilst flags and rosettes were also conspicuous upon them. Chemical Engine Company No. 4 had a neat bower built in front of their shed, upon the top of which a chemical engine was placed, the whole presenting a cheerful appearance. Brown's Hotel, McArthur's, Wallace's and Elvins' stores also showed a variety of handsome decorations.

The Commercial Travellers' Arch was an exceedingly neat and massive piece of work, perfect both in design and workmanship. The centre ran up 35 feet, with streamers bearing the mottoes, "Encourage Commercial, Agricultural, Educational, and Mechanical Enterprises," on one side, and on the other, "Erected by the Commercial Travellers of Belleville." Beneath this was two large piles of trunks and sample cases, good emblems of the fraternity. On the north side stretching across the arch we read, "We sell the Products of the World." On the corners were the words, "Trade and Commerce." The south side across the arch, "Success to the Trade of the City of Belleville." On the corners, "Insurance," "Manufactures." Flags of the nations streamed from every twig. Twenty large panes of stained glass 30x40, running up the sides, made the effect magnificent especially when illuminated. The glass was kindly furnished by Mr. L. W. Yeomans, who has the thanks of the travellers for illuminating the arch. The following are the names of the gentlemen who erected the Commercial Travellers' Arch: Messrs. Niles, Smeaton, Boothe, Wilson, N. McArthur, Geo. McCarthy, Johnson, Phillips, Ellsworthy, Ewin, McIntyre, Hambly, Bradshaw, and Cummins.

A Street Parade in Belleville

     Below this, as far as the junction of Hotel Street,* each one tried to vie with his neighbor in the quantity and style of attractions. The entrance to Roy's brewery was neatly arched and otherwise ornamented. Crothers' office looked "green" and gay; the row of stores continuing south showed off to good advantage, whilst Taylor's jewellery store looked very attractive. The Farmer's Hotel presented a nice front, as did also Brown's, Wilson's and Smith's stores. The attire of the City Hotel, Lockerty's, McCready's and Cook's was quite in keeping with any on the line. Roenigk & Wonnacott showed a fine front, as did also Chapin, Falconer, Linklater and the Empire and Helvetia Hotels. Frost erected a stand in front of his furniture store and displayed a handsome set of furniture; Stewart showed

* Victoria Avenue

21

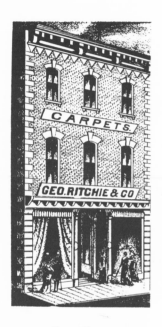

Front Street

that he did not spare time in preparing for this event, as his decorations were quite profuse and varied. Kennedy's building was neatly set off with festoons and Minore's furniture store looked spruce and neat. Yeomans & Co.'s store was very attractive with its flags, festoons and evergreens. O'Neil lent his assistance in the decoration, as did also Jones, Lewis (who showed bunting), and Rous & Co., whose fronts looked fine. The prominent situation occupied by Geen's drug store, and the good taste of its proprietor Ald. Geen, enabled a good display to be made thereat. The appearance of the decorations on the Hotel and Front Street sides was neat and varied, and indicative of good taste. Quite becoming and comparing very favorably with the others, were the attractions of Nulty's, Chown's, Dempsey's, and Chandler's Stores.

The enterprising firm of Geo. Ritchie & Co. erected a beautiful arch in front of their store. The pillars were 24 feet high, and each supplied with a staff, which was provided with a flag. The structure was handsomely decorated with bunting and mottoes; and among other attractions presented the following mottoes: "Welcome to the City of Belleville," and "Fac recte nil time." South of this as far as Bridge Street, the exteriors of the buildings were very becomingly dressed, and showed every evidence of taste as well as the desire to be unexcelled in the manner of their decorations.

On the east side of the street below this point Tickell's store first attracts notice; all the windows in the front of the building are adorned with red, white and blue; flags assist in the ornamentation and evergreens lend a share to the general appearance. Oak Hall front is also decked off, whilst that of Harrison's and Costello's places of business, as well, appear very handsome in their branches of cedar, flags, bunting, &c. One arch covered the entrance to the foot bridge and thus made a continuance of the "green line." Price & Co's, Holton & Co's, and Moynes' all looked nicely in bunting and other devices for display. Walters imitated the example set by his neighbors, and Grant & Potter, in addition to other features, presented an awning framed in green. McKeown continued the line of adornment on his side of the street, whilst Bartman & Seintzel showed off their front in good style. The Anglo-American Hotel and Sutherland's and Fox's made a handsome appearance and in addition to other decorations show any number of small flags. The space from Hambly's saloon to Walker's store inclusive was covered with a grand open awning nicely trimmed and ornamented. Mr. Wm. Johnson in this vicinity made a show of bunting. Glass & Co., Hooey & Son, China Hall and McRae & Co. made a handsome addition to the line of adornment, Watkin also made his contribution, whilst the Consolidated Bank decked its front with little "Jacks." Davenport and Hyman lent their aid to the display, and Mitchell added his contribution in the shape of an awning. Hambly's drug store in its ornamental garb showed to excellent advantage, and Dunnet lighted up his locality with countless flags and bunting. Roblin & Bayeur, Granger, Overell, Haines & Lockett, Warham, Reeves, Mann, Boyce and Morrice presented their fronts in green, and Gillen & Keith on the opposite side of the street made a very fair show. The Robertson Block was one of the very best fronts in the city, for in addition to ornamentation made by the occupants of the several stores on the ground floor — and it is almost superfluous to say, it was excellent — the occupants of the upper parts made contributions in decoration which were very creditable. Take for instance that made by the Odd Fellows, to say the least it was very handsome. The principal ornamentation was the three links — typical of the order — which was a neat specimen of handiwork. The front of the hall of the T.A. of H.C. was also neatly decked and ornamented with flags. Wesley Bullen and Templeton filled out the line to Bridge Street on the east side, and made a very good display. McDonald, in addition to other attractions, showed a number of small jacks and stars and stripes. Hugh Walker was very profuse in his display of evergreens, and McFee, Cummins, and Northgraves continued it. "Long Life and Prosperity to the Citizens of Belleville" appeared on the front of Foster & Reid's. This firm made one of the most attractive displays

Front Street

23

Bridge and Front Streets

on Front Street; over the above named motto was a line of small flags, and in each window of the entire front was a larger flag. There were numbers of pendents and festoons of green neatly trimmed with rosettes of various colors. Three large flags hung from the top of the building, and the Union Jack floated from a staff on the top. Their windows were simply magnificent. Fish & Co. and Spangenberg showed handsome fronts, and Barber, Brignall & Co., in addition to a large display of "handiwork in green," tastefully trimmed and neatly arranged, had a large Union Jack floating from a flag staff on the top of the building, and displayed thereon Barber, Brignall & Co., Importers of dry goods. A double elliptical arch, erected by the city, graced the intersection of Front and Bridge Streets, and was by far the most attractive as well as the most expensive structure of its kind in the city, as well as being a fitting ornament to the locality in which it was erected. The pillars were each 30 feet high, and were topped with a flag pole, from which floated a flag, whilst a long staff projected upwards from the point where the arches crossed one another, and showed thereon the "City of Belleville." From this point a number of lines filled with small flags extended to the posts on the pillars. This arch had the following mottoes upon it "May our City prosper." *Magnum est vectigal parsimonia.* "Industry and Progress" and "God save the Queen." The ornamentation of this structure was of a very elaborate character, and no pains were spared in its decoration. From the base at each corner a small arch stretched to the building adjacent, and these were ornamented with small flags. Festoons of evergreens graced the front of the hall of No. 1 Hose Company, which otherwise looked becomingly attractive.

From this point to the Market Square the decorations were quite extensive on both sides of the street. On the west side, in addition to the display of evergreens, Ross & Davies, Clark, Mrs. Perkins and Greatrix show a large number of flags. The American ensign hung out from the U.S. Consul's office, Pretty and Fuller continued the ornamentation in green, while the office of the *Ontario* presented a well shaded grotto in front of the office with "*Daily Ontario*" in large letters facing the roadway. The display in front of No. 1 Moira Hose Company's Hall compared very favorably with any former exhibit made by that organization. Festoons were suspended from each window and the general front of the building looked very tasty. A streamer which extended from the hall to the City Hall opposite bore the motto "A hearty greeting to our brother firemen." On the east side Clarke & Co.'s store make a neat display, whilst the contribution of the Dominion House was attractive and diffuse, The Grand Central, Leavens Doran and Peterson follow in the lead with a goodly show, and the INTELLIGENCER building presented a very handsome front which was relieved with small flags at frequent intervals. From the arch to the lower bridge the display at either side was good. At the outside of the entrance to the footwalks of the bridge were pillars from which were suspended festoons, which were continued along the girders to the western end, at which point the Temperance associations of the city erected three arches one over each passenger walk and the third over the central portion used for vehicles. The motto "Rescue the Fallen and Support the Weak" appeared at the west side of this arch, and a flag waved from a staff on its summit. The first thing to attract the eye after crossing the bridge is a wheel, suspended in front of McDonald & Birrell's. It was covered with evergreens and looked very tasty. Weese & Coughlin's marble yard was neatly trimmed, as were also the fronts of McGuire's and Harrold's and that of the Windsor Hotel — in front of which a grotto was erected. Lines of evergreens cross the street at this point; Clarke's, Botsford's and H. Yeomans' residences were ornamented, and in front of the residences of Sanford Baker and Ald. Falkiner the display is again resumed and shows itself in festoons and flags. From this to the grounds the decorations are limited, as the number of houses is not large. At M. Ward's and T. O. Bolger's, in addition to other attractions, are Union Jacks and tri-colors. Mr. McCreary made a very nice show, and C. Elliott, Ald. Geen and Rev. R. S. Forneri made a display of evergreens. At the entrance to the grounds was an arch with the motto thereon, "The City Welcomes her Guests."

Around the City Hall, festoons extended to alternate windows, and also from the windows in the belfry, when a number of Union Jacks were also conspicuous. The Street Cars were decorated with evergreens, flags and rosettes, and one car in particular, No. 2, was handsomely ornamented on the inside.

On Hotel Street, between Pinnacle and Church Streets, Dr. Tracey, Miller Empey, E. B. Fraleck, and the Montreal Bank, exhibited a variety of choice decorations, attractively displayed.

The residents of that portion of the City near the intersection of James and Colborne Streets, were apparently determined that all the decorating should not be confined to the line of march and places contiguous to it, and to show that he meant business, Mr. T. Bonner built one of the neatest arches in town at the crossing of the above-named thoroughfares. Three flagpoles supplied with Union Jacks surmounted it, and around the central one was a chandelier with four coal oil lamps, which served for all necessary purposes. The following mottoes appeared upon this structure: "The Day and all who honor it," and "God Save the Queen."

The exhibit from Front to Pinnacle Streets on Bridge Street was very fine, festoons and flags being shown in profusion. On the front of the 15th Batt. Armory, Bogart's Block, and Pitceathly & Kelso's building there was a large show of Union Jacks, and from the latter place across the street a line of bunting was displayed. The windows of La Roche's and Hodgson & Son's offices were arrayed in red, white and blue and Elfis' and the Custom House were nicely decorated. The Dafoe House, in addition to its ornamentation with green and flags, had a bower in front of each door on the Pinnacle and Bridge Street sides, and looked quite holiday-like in its handsome garb. "Success to the City of Belleville" appeared in front of the People's Market, and devices, though of a less expressive kind, were also shown in this quarter. The decorations by Clarke & Co., Green & Co., the Singer Agency, U. E. Thompson's and Lake & Jenkins' were becoming and tasty.

The decorations at the Grand Trunk Station were on quite a large scale, and of a very neat character. There was a goodly display of evergreens, which showed off well. The gardens on either side of the building looked very fine — particularly that on the east side, which appeared very handsome with its variety of flowers in bloom. A small arch was placed over the garden on the west side and a similar one on the east. The emblematic letters V. R. were suspended across the entrance and near the steps in its rear was another small arch. The entrances to the engine sheds were covered with evergreens and the east shop showed a head lamp of a locomotive set off with flags. The western one presented the motto "God Save the Queen." At the entrance to the grounds a very handsome arch 18 feet high was erected by the employees of the company. It displayed a crown, a head lamp of an engine, the Union Jack, a number of small flags and streamers and was otherwise adorned with the mottoes "United we stand, Divided we fall" "Religion, Science, Liberty" "Industry, Integrity, Intelligence." The men who devised and executed this work are worthy of all praise for the manner in which they performed their task. Docter's building looked very well in its suit of green, as did also Mrs. Griffin's. At the head of Bleecker Avenue two streamers of evergreens intertwined, and relieved with bunting stretched from Parrot's to the western engine shed.

Mr. Ellis made a very neat show at his residence; and Mr. Reed lent his aid to the display in the production of two festoons which stretched across the street. Martin's machine shop, Burrell's axe factory and office, and Quinn's and Finnigan's residences were decked in green, as were also the eastern sides of Frost's factory and Lingham's mill on the west side of the river.

Messrs. Campbell & Co's. elevator and store houses were decked with evergreens, as were also some dwellings in that vicinity.

On Campbell street there was a nice show of evergreens in the front of several law offices whilst the fronts of Warham & Diett and Dickens' looked pretty indeed. as did also the Merchants Bank. On the Market square evergreens and flags were largely displayed. The Meat Market was encircled with trees. The City Hall building was festooned and the several fronts from Nicholson's to Richards' was a line of green. "Prosperity to our infant city" shone forth on the front of Cronk's and Howe's boarding, and Kitchen showed his place of business off to advantage.

Arch on Front Street

Several business firms on Front Street, taking advantage of the presence of the multitudes that visited the city, made displays in the windows of their respective places of business. Those made by Foster & Reid and Barber Brignall & Co., were very attractive. Skill, taste and neatness characterized the exhibit, which was one of the finest shown. Fish & Co.'s display was highly creditable, as was also that of S. A. Spangenberg. Harrison's windows were tastefully ornamented, those of the Oak Hall presented a fine appearance; Ritchie & Co's. looked as they always do — handsome; those of Rous & Co. looked splendid, and those of W. Minore presented a nice array of furniture of various kinds.

Throughout the city flags were displayed from staffs at frequent intervals. The National Ensign floated in the breeze from the staff on the City Hall tower, from the Custom House and also from the Court House, and many of the prominent hotels and places of business. The owners of private residences were not behind hand in this regard, for their shows of bunting was good. As a compliment to our American visitors the Stars and Stripes showed itself at intervals, and this made manifest the good will of our people for their friends. In addition to that, at the United States Consulate, three large ones were displayed on Bridge Street, loyally blended with Union Jacks.

THE MORNING PROCESSION.

The procession was the finest of the kind ever seen in Canada, and surpassed in extent and magnificence many of the same nature which we have seen in the largest cities of the United States. An idea of its extent may be formed from the fact that it extended from the Dafoe House, across the market square, along the route to Dundas Street, thence to Charles Street, via Church and Bridge Streets, and occupied over half an hour in passing a given point. The Marshals had a great deal of work to do in managing so large a procession, but finally they succeeded in forming it in the following order:

Grand Marshal Taylor
Band—15th.
15th Batt. Argyle Light Infantry.
49th Hastings Rifles.
The Mayor and Corporation and visitors in carriages.
Chief Engineer and Assistant.
Oddfellows' Band.

Moira Hose Company No. 1.
No. 2 Central Hose, Watertown.
No. 1 Steamer.
35th Batt. Band, Watertown.
No. 1 Neptune Hose, Watertown.
No. 1 Fountain Hose band, Cobourg.
No. 2 Ever Ready Hose, Cobourg.
O. Y. B. band, Port Hope.
No. 2 Independent Hose.
No. 2 Steamer.
No. 3 Quinte Hook and Ladder Company.
No. 4 Active Hose Company.
Grand Encampment Knights of Canada.
The Butchers, led by Capt. Fred Ellis, 20 in number.
The Trades.
Citizens in Carriages.

The route was from the market square by way of Front Street to Dundas, thence to Church, up Church to Bridge; Bridge to Charles; Charles to Hotel; Hotel to Church; Church to Bridge; Bridge to Pinnacle; up Pinnacle to Great St. James; thence around Brown's foundry; down Front Street to the lower bridge, then across the lower bridge, via Bridge Street West, to the Agricultural grounds.

Following is a complete list of the various trades which were represented in the trade procession:

W. R. McRae & Co., grocers, democrat with chests of tea and a hogshead of sugar.

INTELLIGENCER office, double waggon, men at work with press and setting type and distributing extras.

John G. Frost, furniture manufacturer, four horse team, with bales of hay and straw, adorned with flags.

H. McIninch, carriage-maker, four-horse waggon, with men at work in all branches, and cart behind drawing pony to be shod.

G. S. Simpkins, Sewing Machines, single waggon.

Bell & Co., similar turnout.

Brown & St. Charles, carriage maker, four horse waggon with men at work.

H. Corby & Sons, millers and distillers, four horse waggon, with barrels of liquors, piled upon which were bags of corn-meal, the whole surmounted by small union jacks.

Mrs. Tugnett, milliner, four-horse waggon, with several milliners at work — a very fine display.

P. Hambly, baker, single waggon, decorated with flags.

Bay of Quinte Steam Brick Works, one four horse and four double waggons, with workmen busy at work and a steam engine in operation — the whole preceded by Messrs. Holden and Foster in a carriage.

G. S. Tickell, furniture manufacturer, two double and a four horse waggon, with mechanics illustrating the process of manufacture.

McDonald & Birrell, carriage makers, single buggy.

J. M. Walker & Co., founders and implement makers, threshing machine.

N. Lingham, City Brick Works, a double waggon, with men at work manufacturing.

J. F. Marshall, horticulturist, single waggon with a fine display of flowers.

James Roy, brewer, double waggon with kegs of beer, surmounted by a bale of hops.

Hop culture was illustrated by N. Lingham with a double waggon well filled with hops and neatly ornamented.

Agriculture was illustrated by four produce merchants in a carriage, with sheaves of grain.

Cronk's parcel express, conveying a quantity of goods ready for delivery.

Muir & Lawrance, hatters and furriers, double waggon with a display of hats and furs, surmounted by a deer.

Daily Ontario, double waggon, with a Gordon press and several men at work, and distributing supplements.

J. A. Brock & Co., photographers, double waggon, with implements of the art, and a handsome female "subject" seated.

G. L. McCornock, double waggon, with Wheeler & Wilson sewing machines.

G. & J. Brown, three double waggons with a splendid display of ploughs and various other implements of their own manufacture.

W. Severn, brewer, double waggon with barrels of ale.

Parade

Northcott & Alford, carpenters and builders, double waggon, with mechanics working.

Belleville Marble works, Weese & Coughlin, double waggon with a number of men busily employed.

H. Wilkins, double waggon, with specimen of his manufacture in artificial stone.

James Barrett, two double waggons, with sewing machines of his well-known manufacture, also single waggon with organ.

W. Powell, double waggon with platform on which were velocipedes of his own manufacture.

A. Hodgson & Son, cheese buyers, three waggons with "Hodgson's a No. 1 cheese."

Also a single waggon load of "Higgins Eureka salt."

John G. Frost, double waggon with several mechanics manufacturing furniture.

J. C. Stewart, boot and shoemaker, a four horse and a two horse waggon, with men illustrating the process of manufacture. On the leading teams of the four horse waggon were outriders in the gayest of dresses.

B. Pashley and H. Kleingbeil, milk waggons.

E. Burrell, axe maker, four horse waggon with outriders, a number of men working at all the processes of manufacture.

Flint & Holton, sash, door and blind manufacturers, a four and a two horse waggon, giving a fine exhibit of their manufactures and of the process of manufacture from the log onwards. This firm were very unfortunate in that a big waggon conveying their planing machine and matching machine, with a steam engine, broke down on Bridge Street near the Dafoe House.

The above list includes, we have reason to believe, all the

exhibits which were made by the various trades, and we only regret that lack of space prevents detail, as some of the turnouts were truly magnificent.

The military made a fine display, the Knights of Canada were out in strong force and attracted much attention, and the butchers, well mounted, caparisoned in the neatest manner, and led by Captain Alfred Ellis, were much admired.

The route was thronged with many thousands of people, all of whom were delighted with the extent and magnificence of the procession, which, with the many colored uniforms of the firemen and military, the waving banners and the fine music of the bands was a sight never to be forgotten. The one great drawback was the intense heat, but a general use of umbrellas, the deep shade of the trees with which the streets are lined, and a cooling breeze which sprung up did much to mitigate its effects, although some light cases of sun stroke took place both amongst the spectators and in the ranks of the procession.

On arrival at the grounds the Marshals gave an exhibition of horsemanship, in which Messrs. Thompsons's, Clute's and Flint's horses cleared the jumps beautifully, but strange to say Mr. Lloyd's "Viley," the most celebrated hurdle jumper in Canada, unaccountably refused the water jump.

THE INAUGURAL ADDRESS.

The Mayor and visitors having taken the stand, the Mayor expressed his great satisfaction at the success of the demonstration, and expressed warm thanks to the citizens for contributing so largely to that result. He called upon the Hon. Billa Flint to deliver the inaugural address, warmly eulogizing Mr. Flint as an old and respected citizen, who had lived here 49 years and had been identified with our progress and prosperity, and had been honored with the highest position which it was in the power of the government to bestow.

Hon. Billa Flint

Hon. Mr. Flint, on coming forward, was received with cheers and applause. He spoke in substance as follows, after making a few introductory remarks:

My first recollection of Belleville goes back to the war between England and the United States in 1812-15; at that time it was called Meyers' Creek, Captain Walter Meyers being then a prominent man in the place. The land around the town plot reserved by the Government being owned by Captain Meyers and others.

The present name Belleville was given to the place about the close of the war in honor of Lady Belle Gore, wife of Governor Gore. The original Town plot was surveyed in 1816.

After the war was over little was known by me of Belleville until the first steamer commenced running in 1818 from the Carrying Place to Prescott, under the command of the late Henry Gildersleeve, of Kingston. The steamer regularly called at my father's wharf in Brockville, for freight and passengers, as also for the Captain to sell us flour and eggs, which for years he brought down from Belleville for exchange for cash or sometimes for salt in the barrel. This trade commenced in the fall of 1818, which traffic continued up to June, 1829. The *Charlotte* was a very slow boat, with under-deck cabin which would accommodate six ladies and twelve gentlemen for sleeping purposes.

My first trip to Belleville was in May, 1822, with a lot of lumber waggons to sell, time from Brockville two days and one night. I found a striking contrast between the two places, Belleville being a dirty dilapidated looking place sparsely settled, and after a rain storm mud half knee deep.

There was one small church, St. Thomas. I heard of no other. I think the Methodists worshipped in a large room at that time. I was here again in the Fall of 1822, not much improvement to be seen from Spring, there were two grist mills with rock stone, two saw mills with one upright saw each, one carding and fulling mill, run by J. E. Sleeper, several small stores and public houses, the best of which was kept by Old Mr. Nelson, on the site where the Mayor's new block of stores now stands, east side of Front Street. Very little paint was to be seen on the buildings at that time.

In 1829 I came to Belleville and rented a place to commence business, there were sixteen stores when I came, (one of our large stores at present contains more worth of goods than the whole sixteen did at that time). The old "Charlotte" had given place to a new steamer called the "Sir James Kemp," also commanded by the late Captain Gildersleeve, it was a more commodious, and somewhat faster boat than the "Charlotte." There was another steamer called the "Toronto." This boat was built of plank and was sharp at both bow and stern, and was for a time commanded by the late Captain Henry Baldwin, who about that time gave command

St. Thomas Church

Upper Bridge
c. 1875

to his son. These steamers each made one trip from the Carrying Place to Prescott, and one to Kingston each week, very few schooners were seen here at that time.

There was one "Durham Boat" which made trips from all parts of the Bay to Montreal in the spring and fall and was owned and commanded by the late Harry Fanning, of Sidney, there was no market at that time, no ditches or drains for carrying off the water from the streets, no improvements made in either grist or saw mills except an extra saw mill on the west side of the river called Bleecker's mill, and one dilapidated School House sitting in a mud hole in rainy weather, more fit for a pigpen than a place to teach children in, one brick and two wooden churches, all small, one carding and fulling machine, and several public houses, and 700 inhabitants.

There are but one male and six female resident house-holders left of all there were when I came here, Mr. James Wilson being the only male who stands ahead of me, and so great a change has taken place in the then population of Belleville in the past forty-nine years that very few of the younger branches of that day are to be found in the City at this time. The people had to go to Kingston to attend all the Courts, except the old Division Court for suits under $8, the legal profession had good pickings in those days.

In 1836 a Board of Police was elected comprising five members. Of that board I am the only one remaining, all the others having gone to their long home.

Court House

That year we built stone sidewalks on Front street to the wharves, as also as near as practicable to the various churches. The stone sidewalks have since given place to plank walks.

In the winter of 1837 the first steam saw mill commenced operations with one muley saw and two small circulars, and in the fall some sawn lumber was sent by schooner to Oswego. That fall the Rebellion broke out and the Town was soon filled with volunteers on duty, giving the Town a military appearance until spring, the same took place in 1838.

In 1841 the Court House and Gaol was finished and Belleville proclaimed the County Town for Hastings, a grand illumination and great rejoicing followed.

In 1849 by Act of Parliament the Town limits were enlarged to 1285 acres, and divided into four wards, namely, Sampson, Baldwin, Ketcheson and Coleman Wards, which were named by me after four of the most prominent persons residing in the Town. A market was first established that year.

In 1850 the Board of Police was changed to a Town Council, consisting of twelve members, the late Benjamin F. Davy was elected Mayor, population 2,840 or an increase of four to one in twenty years. The trade of the Town had quadrupled now and better buildings had been erected and old ones repaired, some small manufactories had been started.

In 1859 the Mayor was first elected by the popular vote, the choice fell on the late Francis McAnnany, which system continued until 1878.

In 1874, there was a change in the Town limits from 1,285 to 1,495 acres, and seven Wards, fourteen members besides the Mayor.

In 1877 the population having increased as per census to 11,192, the Lieutenant-Governor of Ontario by proclamation, in December, declared Belleville to be a City after the 31st of that month, and our first civic elections took place in January last, when 21 Aldermen were elected, and Alexander Robertson, Esq., was elected first City Mayor.

Belleville has grown slowly but surely, and to-day bids fair to go on and prosper, it is not possible to give more than a condensed account. There are many incidents which would be of great interest to the reader were it possible to publish them in order from time to time, as they occurred since my moving to Belleville in 1829, but neither time or space will permit, nor is it necessary to enumerate the improvements in buildings or otherwise, our County Buildings, High School and Common Schools, numerous Churches, Factories, Mills, splendid Merchants' Shops and palatial private residences all speak for themselves, while the increase in our steamers and sailing vessels has been large and our exports and imports show the volume of our trade. Forty-nine years ago the imports were principally of American salt fifty cents per barrel. Our exports were small, in fact none.

Redick & Farley's Planing Mills

Lower Front Street
c. 1880

The following is a statement of our Exports and Imports, of various years, illustrating the increase since 1850:—

In 1850	Exports	$245,693	Imports	$116,363
1860	"	400,000	"	172,949
1870	"	587,834	"	155,231
1873	"	739,500	"	247,867
1877	"	333,223	"	273,505

The falling off in exports from 1873 to 1877 is owing to the decrease in the lumber trade.

The hon. gentleman concluded his address with an eloquent eulogy of our country, predicting a brilliant future for the City of Belleville.

THE GAMES.

Shortly after the hour named, the programme of Caledonian Games was proceeded with, under the direction of Chief McKinnon. The crowd, at first small in number, rapidly increased until at least 4,000 people were present and looking on as interested spectators. As we anticipated, the keen competition produced some of the most exciting struggles, and the best previous record beaten in more than one instance. That grand athlete Mr. E. W. Johnson, of Hamilton, made the best running hop, step and jump on record, namely, 45 ft. 1 inch, and also made 5 ft. 1 inch in the standing high jump, which he could have exceeded, if desired. Of the local men, Mr. E. F. Millburn made a splendid exhibition in the pole leaping, being although without training, beaten only one inch by one of the best professionals, and dividing second and third with another of them. With a little practice he would have won easily. Mr. W. Robertson also nobly upheld the reputation of Belleville. Mr. McGillivray, of Montreal, although an amateur, also performed very finely, whilst the professionals generally excelled themselves on the occasion. Following is a return of the sports:—

The opening was a Threesome reel by Messrs. Matthewson, Robertson, and Henderson, of Hamilton, in Highland costume,

which was much admired, and heartily applauded. The programme was then proceeded with, the names of the competitors being as follows:

Putting the heavy stone, 21 lbs. — 1st, Jas. McGillivray, Montreal, 34 ft. 2 in.; 2nd, E. W. Johnson, Hamilton, 33 ft. 10; 3rd, — Harrison, Toronto, 32 ft. 11 in. Exhibition throws of Harrison, 36 ft. 1 in.

Putting the light stone, 14 lbs. — 1st,. E. W. Johnson, 44 ft. 11 in.; 2d, — Harrison, 42 ft. 4 in.; James McGillivray, 40 ft. 3 in.

Exhibition throws by Chief McKinnon, 45 ft. and 51 ft.

Standing long jump — 1st, E. W. Johnson, 10 ft. 1 in.; 2d, Robt. Rankin, 9 ft. 11 in.; 3d, Smith, Cobourg, 9 ft. 9 in.

Reel of Tulloch in Highland Costume — 1st, G. Mathewson; 2d, Henderson.; 3d, George Robertson, all of Hamilton.

Short Race, 100 yards — 1st, E. W. Johnson, 11¼ sec.; 2d, A. C. Reid; 3d, — Irvine, Ottawa.

Vaulting with the Pole — 1st, Smith 10 ft. 1 in.; 2d and 3d, E. F. Milburn and Brady of Toronto, tied at 10 ft. and divided.

Running Jump — 1st, A. C. Reid, Hamilton, 21 ft. 3 in.; 2nd, E. W. Johnson, 19 ft. 10 in.; 3rd, Jas. McGillivray, 19 ft. 6 in.

Sword Dancing — 1st, Mathewson; 2d, Henderson; 3d, Robertson.

Running Hop, Step and Jump — 1st, E. W. Johnson, 45 ft. 1 in.; 2d, John Mahoney, Montreal, 40 ft. 4 in.; 3d, J. Boyd, 40 ft. 3 in.

Standing High Jump — 1st, F. W. Johnson, 5 ft. 1 in.; 2d, W. J. Phoenix, Norham, 5 ft.; Smith and Rankin tied and divided 3d prize.

Running High Jump — 1st, E. W. Johnson, 6 ft. 0½ in.; 2nd,

39

and 3rd, J. McGillivray and A. C. Reid, 6 ft. 0½ in. and the prize was divided.

Strathspey and Reel — 1st, Mathewson; 2d Henderson; 3d, Robertson.

200 yards Hurdle Race — 1st, A C. Reid; 2d, Irvine; 3d, Nelson.

Throwing heavy hammer — 1st Brady, 82 ft.; 2nd Johnson, 76 ft.; 3rd Harrison, 75 ft. Chief McKinnon, exhibition throw, 89 ft.

Throwing light hammer — 1st, Brady, 94 ft.; 2nd Johnson, 87 ft. 9; 3rd, Harrison, 87 ft. Chief McKinnon, exhibition throw with one hand, 107 ft. 10 in.

Mile race — 1st, Irvine; 2d, O. Dyas; 3d, G. W. Shears. Time 5 min. 35 sec.

Quarter mile race — 1st Johnson; 2d, Reid; 3d, W. Robertson, Belleville.

One mile walking race — 1st, Irvine; 2d, Shears; 3rd, Beesley. Time 8 min.

Tossing the caber — 1st, Johnson, 37 ft. 6 in.; 2nd, Brady, 36 ft. 7 in.

Bagpipe playing Pibroch and March — Geo. A. Smith, Hamilton.

Three hand reel — 1st, Matthewson; 2nd, Henderson; 3d, Robertson.

The Sack race did not fill.

Quoits — 1st, Alexander Robertson; 2d, E. Hayne; 3d, John Taylor.

Boys' race — 1st, M. McMullen; 2d, 3d, H. Beesley, all of Belleville.

The various bands on the grounds played at intervals, adding much to the interest and enjoyment of the occasion. All were delighted with the games, which are destined to become very popular here, and in which on a future occasion we have no doubt that many of our local men will excel, as they now know the value of careful training. The Chief, who showed his pre-eminence yesterday, will doubtless have still more pupils to introduce to the public when next athletic games take place in Belleville.

THE BANQUET.

Our report of this event is unavoidably deferred until tomorrow's issue.

THE TORCHLIGHT PROCESSION.

Shortly after 8 o'clock the firemen began to assemble on the market square, and after some excellent music by the bands, including "Yankee Doodle" and the British national anthem, the torches were lighted and the line of march taken up. The sight was a grand one, and it was something wonderful to see the dense crowds which turned out to witness it. One of Prof. Hand's assistants discharged a quantity of beautiful fireworks in front of the procession as it passed along, and as the hour was now getting late the route was shortened and the procession passed on quickly to the Agricultural grounds.

THE ILLUMINATIONS.

The display made in the evening was a fitting conclusion to the proceedings of the day. Front Street in many places was grandly illuminated and presented a beautiful sight and as many of the private residences were handsomely lighted up, the effect was beautiful, the scene perfect and the throngs that filled the streets could not but be pleased with the grandeur the sight afforded. In front of the hall of Moira Hose Company No. 1 a beautiful sight presented itself and called forth universal expressions of admiration. A large number of gas jets formed in the letters "V.R." and also in the name "Moira Hose No. 1" produced a fine effect. The windows of the hall were covered with red, white and blue, and the interior of the hall being well lighted, a beautiful sight presented itself. In front of the City Hall, and extending from one street to the other, was a semi-circle of gas jets which showed up brilliantly. Chinese lanterns adorned the front of the *Ontario* office and Mr. Pretty's residence, and also Mrs. Perkins's, Knox's, and Clark's. The INTELLIGENCER building was set off to considerable advantage by the appearance, at each window, of a lantern, whilst Leavens' store, the Grand Central, and the Dominion House, made contributions in the same way. A line of lanterns stretched across the street at the Dominion Telegraph office; there was also a number of the same contrivances at Ellis' butcher shop and at Dr. Willson's residence. Rev. Mr. Burke's residence presented a very beautiful appearance, as the interior of the building was brilliantly illuminated, and a number of lanterns in the grounds produced a pleasing effect. At McIninch's and Lattimer's, on Church St., lights were also shown, and at E. W. Holton's, Nathan Jones', Henry Corby's jr., H. Corby, sen., and U. E. Thompson, and other lanterns of various styles and sizes displayed. At the residence of Mr. Bowell, M.P., there was a very large exhibit of lanterns suspended at frequent intervals among the trees, and produced a very pretty scene. The grounds in front of Col. Baker's looked beautiful with many lights, whilst the numberless brilliancies in front of George Wallbridge's residence, made the scene in that locality a grand one. Mr. Alexander Brown's residence was finely lighted up in the interior, and the lawns in front of Mr. F. Clarke's, Mr. Brenton's, Mr. Nosworthy's and Mrs. Furnival's were nicely illuminated. The residence of John Lewis showed off to good advantage, the lights in the tower being conspicuous at a considerable distance. Lanterns were also noticeable at Ald. Price's, Mr. Maunder's, G.C. Holton's, Mayor Robertson's, Farley's, S. S. Wallbridge's, Soper's, Reynolds' and Forin's. The illumination at Col. Hulme's was very pretty and the "lighted" motto "Prosperity to our City" shone forth to nice advantage. Dr. Tracy's was handsomely lighted both on the interior and exterior and the front of the Montreal Bank and Mr. Dougall's presented a splendid appearance. A row of lanterns adorned the Front and Bridge Streets sides of the roof of the building at the north east corner, and Foster & Reid's store looked very cheerful and pretty in its varied illuminations. The Oddfellows' Hall was handsomely lighted whilst lanterns in front of Dunnett's, Roblin & Bayeur's, China Hall, and Johnson's produced a good effect. McRae & Co's. front shone forth in red, white and blue as did also that of G. S. Tickell whilst that of Glass & Co. presented a beautiful sight, as in large letters formed by innumerable jets of gas the words "Belleville Gas Co's Office," "Hardware" and "James Glass & Co.," appeared and on the top of the building was a number of jets of gas encircled with globes. The exhibit was the finest in the city, and was a very pleasing and attractive sight to passers by. Lanterns were prominent objects in front of Grant & Potter's, Costello's, Stewart's, Frost's, and Elvins' stores, and O'Brien's hotel. Lockerty's residence was also nicely lighted. The illumination of the Commercial Travellers' arch was grand, the many colored lights producing a beautiful effect, and showing off the structure to excellent advantage. The greater number of the prominent stores on Front Street were also lighted, which made them appear cheerful and bright.

The festoons on the lower bridge were hung with large numbers of Chinese lanterns, and a fine display was made on the west side of the river.

Mr. Tugnett had brilliant lights blazing from his chimney, and Mr. James Harold's residence was brightly illuminated.

At Mr. J. W. Loudon's, corner of Colborne and James Streets, a number of Chinese lanterns were hung in the trees, lighting up the neighborhood nicely.

At Mr. Botsford's there was a brilliant illumination in parti-colors. At Clark's grocery a number of Chinese lanterns were displayed, whilst Mr. Horace Yeomans' residence was handsomely illuminated and a large number of Chinese lanterns were hung in the trees.

At Miss Ponton's the house was illuminated, and at Mr. Sandford Baker's the festoons were hung with Chinese lanterns.

The Murney residence was illuminated, and trees and shrubbery thinly hung with Chinese lanterns, making a beautiful display. Rev. Mr. Burton's dwelling and grounds were beautifully lit up, as were also those of Messrs. M. D. Ward, Thos. O. Bolger, A. Shearing, Alderman Geen, C. F. Elliott, B. Walker, and a number of others on Bridge Street, the whole forming a rarely beautiful scene, such as is rarely witnessed.

THE FIREWORKS.

The culmination of the celebration was the exhibition of fireworks at the Agricultural Grounds by Prof. Hand, of Hamilton. If the crowd in the afternoon had been great, that at night was simply enormous, the number of persons who thronged the enclosure being estimated by many competent judges at from 10,000 to 12,000. Certainly it was the largest gathering that ever took place on those grounds. Expectation as to the quality of this display had run very high, but it was more than equalled, the extent and magnificence of the exhibition being such as had never been witnessed here before, whilst the night was calm and favorable. A better description than is contained in the programme it would not be possible to give, therefore we refer the reading to the Professor's own account of the display, as published.

It had been arranged that music should be furnished by the bands, but for some reason no musical performance was given.

The fireworks display being over, the crowd thronged to the

gates, at which a tremendous jam occurred, but fortunately no one was hurt in the "squeeze," though some people were jammed considerably. Thus, so far as the Corporation was concerned, the festivities came to a close at about 11 o'clock p.m.

NO. 2's ASSEMBLY.

Independent Hose Co. No. 2 held an assembly in the City Hall immediately following the conclusion of the display of fireworks. There was a very large attendance, and "all went merry as a marriage bell" until the departure of the visitors, the Watertown men leaving at 2 a.m., and the Cobourg visitors half an hour later. This assembly was one of the most enjoyable events of the day.

LACROSSE

Two interesting matches took place on the old cricket ground, between clubs representing Napanee, Picton, and this City. The game between the Alerts and the Napanee club resulted in a tie after four games had been played, two being taken by each club. The fifth was undecided, and therefore the game was declared a draw. In the contest between the Oka and Picton clubs, the home team was successful, winning 3 out of 4 games. C. Sherwood was fortunate in each instance in putting the ball through the visitor's goal. Each of the above games was witnessed by a large number of spectators.

NOTES.

Some slight cases of sun-stroke occurred, but fortunately the medical men were on hand and treated them promptly and successfully.

No accidents to life or limb were reported.

It is very creditable to all concerned that there was so little drunkenness. Less than half a dozen arrests were made.

A child was knocked down by a fractious horse, but was not seriously hurt.

Some small fires occurred amongst the evergreens from the Chinese lanterns, but all were promptly extinguished.

It was pleasing news to hear of the success of the Belleville yachts at Kingston — *Kathleen* first and *Katie Gray* second.

Chief McKinnon is the proudest man in town to-day. His favorite games, although decried beforehand by some, hit the popular fancy, and his favorite pupil E. W. Johnson stood first in the games.

Congratulations "all round" — to Aldermen, citizens and all concerned — on the great success of the day, which was unmarred by any untoward occurrence.

Mr. H. J. Lott's horse took a carnivorous turn yesterday afternoon and ran into Green & Co's butcher shop. Damage slight.

A number of letters of apology for their absence were received from heads of municipalities who found it impossible to attend, by Alderman D. B. Robertson Secretary of the General Committee on the Demonstration.

Other local news is crowded out to make room for the very full account of the demonstration.

The great arch, corner of Front and Bridge Streets, is to be illuminated to-night, as will also be that at the Grand Trunk.

A pickpocket was captured yesterday when plying his vocation.

Photographic artists were busy photographing the decorations to-day.

THE CITY OF BELLEVILLE

Grand Inaugural Celebration

THE DEMONSTRATION A COMPLETE SUCCESS

THE BANQUET

This event took place in the evening at 7:30 at the Dafoe House, and was a happy continuance of the day's proceedings. The spacious dining hall of the establishment was appropriately decorated for the occasion; festoons of evergreens were suspended from the chandeliers and mottoes of various significations encircled the room. "God Save the Queen" was conspicuous at the head, "May our Country Prosper" adorned the foot of the room, whilst on the sides were "Success to our Industry," "May our City Prosper," "Welcome to our Guests," and "Economy and Prosperity." Miniature Union Jacks and Stars and Stripes commingling made the scene a pleasant one.

At the head of the table sat His Worship Mayor Robertson, supported on his right by Mayor Deacon, of Lindsay, and Messrs. Ferris and Striker, M.P.P.'s. On his left were Mayor Henry and Superintendent Lindley, of Brantford, and Mayor Toole, of Peterboro, Aldermen Bergeman and Barber, of Watertown, N. Y., some of our City Aldermen, and a number of prominent residents of this locality were also present. Ald. Robertson filled the duties of the Vice-chair satisfactorily. The Band of the 15th Batt. A. L. 1. lent a helping hand, and at frequent intervals discoursed a number of pleasing selections. The tables were plentifully furnished with all that the appetite could wish for, and a corps of attentive and obliging assistants lent their endeavors to supply the wants of the guests.

After the good things provided had been disposed of, the Mayor rose and remarked that as some of the guests were going away and as those present wished to witness the fireworks and torchlight procession, it became necessary to abbreviate the list of toasts and make the speeches as short as possible so as to accomplish that end. He expressed his satisfaction with the result of the demonstration, which he considered had been very successful; it was indeed a proud day for the city — it was a proud day for him as its Mayor, and he felt a just pride in the success of the inauguration of the city. The excellent manner in which the programme had been carried out was not alone attributable to the efforts of the members of the Council, but to those citizens who nobly came forward and lent valuable assistance in beautifying our streets and giving the place its handsome appearance. They built arches and they decorated their dwellings in a very pretty manner. Several had come forward and, with their own means, built handsome structures to adorn the streets. Corby & Sons, Ritchie & Co., W. Y. Mikel and the Commercial Travellers erected arches at their own expense, and he was pleased to know that they, as well as numbers of others (the ladies included), lent such valuable aid in decorating the city. He was sure it was a proud day for the city, and felt confident that if our forefathers could have been present to see the march of improvement that had been manifested here, they would return not only confused, but astounded with the improvements that have been made. The other events of the evening would now cause him to draw his speech to a close. He would now call upon them to drink a toast — one which he felt confident would be received in a loyal manner. He gave "The Queen," a mother whose model should be copied in every land; may she long live. She had already reigned 41 years and he only trusted that she might long continue to reign.

The toast was drunk amid rounds of applause, the company standing, whilst the band played "God Save the Queen."

The Mayor remarked that the next toast he would give referred to our neighbors across the lines. Years ago gentlemen took exception to their mode of government, others had faith in it and eventually came to this country and settled here. The former succeeded in creating a republic second to none on the face of the globe, and although they are now advancing and progressing we are endeavoring to keep pace with them. The toast he would give was "long life, health and prosperity to the President of the United States."

The band, "Yankee Doodle."

Mr. E. N. Bergeman, on being called upon, invoked the assistance of Mr. McGregor, who spoke of the "welcomes" extended in his progress through the city. These welcomes suited him, and he "took them in." He paid a glowing tribute to the display made on the streets; spoke approvingly of the interest taken in the celebration by our citizens; and gave expression to the sentiment that the "Queen might long continue to reign." He trusted that the differences and prejudices which existed between the United States and Canada would soon disappear, and that they might become more brotherly as time advanced. On behalf of the officers of the Watertown firemen, he extended his heartfelt thanks for the cordial welcome extended, and he felt assured that if he were to enter a strange place and found that his entertainment was of a pleasing character, he would say that he was in Belleville. Again thanking the citizens for the honor conferred by inviting the Watertown firemen to be present, and extending them thanks for hospitalities received, he took his seat amid loud applause.

The Mayor, in a very fitting and appropriate speech, gave the "Governor General," which was heartily received.

The next toast was "The Army, Navy, and Volunteers."

Band — "British Grenadiers."

Lt.-Col. Deacon replied. He said it was a pleasure to him to be called on to reply to the toast, and expressed the gratification it afforded him to reply to this toast especially, as he had formerly been connected with the British army, and now with the Canadian Volunteers. He paid a compliment to the City on its holiday appearance, and remarked that although our girls were handsome, those of his own town (Lindsay,) would in his opinion not lead him to think they should take a back seat. Returning to his subject, he spoke of the loyalty of the volunteers, and expressed his confidence in their patriotism and devotion. After returning thanks for the kindness extended him, and through him to the people of Lindsay for the invitation, he resumed his seat amid applause.

Col. Brown, Col. Lazier and John White, Esq., M.P., also replied to this toast in fitting terms. The mayor remarked that a great deal of our success in the celebration was attributed to persons residing at a distance. Some had come a long way to unite with us and assist us today, and therefore as a tribute to them, he would propose the toast of "Our Guests," coupled with the name of Mayor Henry of Brantford.

Mayor Henry expressed the pleasure afforded him at being present on this occasion, and returned his thanks for the welcome and kindness extended him. He came here on Saturday night; he had looked around the city; admired its streets and avenues, and trusted that it would go on and prosper. Brantford was ahead of Belleville in the matter of streets, but the latter was ahead of Brantford in the matter of shade trees. He never saw in any city a greater number of fine ladies than he saw in the city today. He hoped Belleville would follow Brantford in all that was good, and trusted our city would go on and prosper.

In conclusion, he gave "The Mayor and Corporation of the City of Belleville."

Mayor Robertson replied. After a few passing remarks, he went on to speak of the programme of the celebration, which he received from Brantford. Of the inaugural it was a perfect success, and to the Aldermen in general, and to D. B. Robertson in particular, was the success of today's entertainment attributable. He called on that gentleman to reply.

Mr. Robertson expressed his regret at the absence of many of the Aldermen whom he considered should have been here on this occasion. He was pleased to notice the presence around the festive board of the Mayors of Peterboro and Lindsay and was certain their presence was an augury of success. He spoke of the difficulties which the Grand Junction Railway had experienced and the results that would follow from its construction and felt confident that when it would be completed it would be of great advantage and benefit to Lindsay and Peterboro and our own city as well. He had worked for the success of the inaugural day; he always worked when he was called upon to do anything, and he now felt proud of the success of the celebration. He concluded by proposing the health of the Mayor and Corporation of Peterboro.

Mayor Toole replied. He spoke of the rapid progress of Belleville and the enterprise shown by its inhabitants, and was gratified with both. With reference to the Grand Junction Railway, he only trusted that the distance between his town and the City of Belleville would be lessened in time, and he was confident that with the presentation of just and equitable terms to his people they would largely contribute toward the Grand Junction. He would be glad to meet any deputation that would be sent to Peterboro to attain that end, and was confident any application made would receive a favorable consideration.

Mayor Deacon, of Lindsay, made a few remarks on the same subject, after which the proceedings terminated.

NOTES

In the hurry of preparing so lengthy a report as that of the civic demonstration, errors *will* creep in and omissions occur in spite of the utmost care. For instance, the display of chinese lanterns at the Murney Mansion is spoken of as "thinly" hung amongst the trees and shrubbery, whereas it should have been "thickly." The standing long jump of E. W. Johnson is given as 10 ft 1 inch, whereas it should have been 10 inches more. The hitch and kick competition was accidentally omitted. It should have been inserted as follows:

Hitch and Kick — 1st, A. C. Reid, 8 ft. 11 in.; 2nd, E. W. Johnston, 8 ft. 10 in.; 3rd Smith.

The display of flags at the Canadian Bank of Commerce, also the decorations at the house of Mr. Robert Thomson, manager of that institution, accidentally escaped notice.

The great arch was not lit up last night owing to the accidental displacement of some of the lanterns.

The handsome arch at the Grand Trunk Railway Station was beautifully illuminated last night. The locomotive head light in the centre made a brilliant illumination, whilst the arch was thickly hung with signal lights — red, green and white — and a number of Chinese lanterns. The sight was a very pretty one, and its beauty was enhanced by the exhibition of head lights on the engine sheds. A large crowd witnessed the pleasing display. The Oddfellows' band was, it was understood, to have given a performance, and Mr. Gunn, the obliging Station Agent, had the sidewalks sprinkled and seats placed on a platform car for the band, which for some reason, did not appear, greatly to the regret of the assembled hundreds.

The bell of St. Michael's church rang merrily for an hour on Monday morning, in welcome to the visitors to the city, and from the spire and other points of vantage floated the Union Jack and other flags.

Many people are now taking down the decorations from their premises, and the festival may be said to be over.

We learn from Mr. Allan McFee that the Oddfellows' band had no notice as to playing at the station last night.

Notices of the decorations at H. Cronk's on Pinnacle Street and Nathan Jones', Front Street, were accidentally omitted, and it was Mr. F. Frost, and not Mr. Jno. G. Frost, on whose wagon furniture manufacturing was being carried on.

Town Council, 1877

Simpson's Tavern

Historic Belleville

Belleville had its beginning following the close of the American Revolution when a number of United Empire Loyalists came to settle in Upper Canada.

Among the first to take up permanent residence at the site of the present city at the mouth of the Moira on the Bay of Quinte, was Captain George Singleton, a Loyalist from New York Province. He opened a fur trading post in partnership with his brother-in-law, Lieutenant Isaac Ferguson, on the east bank of the river in 1784. For a time the settlement was known as Singleton's Creek. Both Singleton and Ferguson died in 1789 and shortly after their place as the settlement's leading merchants was taken by Captain John Walden Meyers.

Captain Meyers who had served with the Loyalist forces during the American Revolution, came to Thurlow Township in 1790 and built the first grist mill on the Moira River. For several years it was the only mill between Napanee to the east and York (Toronto) to the west. Soon Captain Meyers' enterprises included a sawmill, a trading post and a distillery. Today, on the east bank of the river still stand the remains of the Captain's

The Original St. Andrew's Church

Wallbridge House
Dundas and Front Streets

mill. He also operated a brick kiln and in 1794 erected on a hill overlooking the Moira, what is considered to have been the first brick house in Upper Canada.

Meyers' industries soon attracted other settlers and a village began to form some distance below the mill at the river's mouth. The settlement was known as Meyers' Creek until 1816. That year the village was surveyed by Samuel G. Wilmot who found already some fifty homes, stables and other buildings clustered around Simpson's Tavern, which had been opened on the southwest corner of Dundas and Front Streets in 1798. The population at the time was one hundred and fifty. A post office was established in 1816 with Simon McNabb as the first postmaster, and the village officially assumed the name of Belleville after Lady Bella Gore who with her husband provincial Lieutenant-Governor Francis Gore, had stopped at the settlement on their way to York (Toronto) that year.

In 1836 Belleville was incorporated as a police village. Billa Flint, a prominent businessman, was elected as the first President of the Board of Police, a position equivalent to that of mayor. The other members of the board, or council, were: William McCarthy, Asa Yeomans, Zenas Dafoe and William Connor.

Belleville rapidly developed into a bustling lumber centre and became a town in 1850 with Benjamin Davy as the first mayor. The population by then had reached 2,200. In 1860 the town was separated from the County of Hastings for municipal purposes.

By the time Belleville was incorporated as a city in 1878 the population had risen to more than eleven thousand. Alexander Robertson served as the new city's first mayor. W. J. Diamond, one of the aldermen at the time and in later years mayor, designed the city's coat of arms. Although never officially registered, it has been in continued use until now.

The Old Pinnacle St. Church

City Hall, a proud landmark and, with its graceful tower, one of the finest examples of Gothic architecture, was built five years before Belleville was incorporated as a city. On Christmas Eve, 1873, the four clock faces of the tower were lit up with gas jets for the first time.

Belleville's first schoolhouse was a crude log cabin built around 1809 below the market near the river. John Watkins was the teacher. In 1816 the community formed its first school board. Although several private schools operated in Belleville during the early years, common schools remained few until after the Common School Act was passed in the late 1840's making primary education free and compulsory for all. By 1860 Belleville had five primary schools managed by a board of eight trustees.

The first County Grammar School was erected on Church Street in Belleville in the 1840's. It was one of only a few secondary schools then in existence in the province of Ontario. Alexander Burdon was the first headmaster.

Lower Bridge
c. 1875

The Belleville Seminary founded by members of the Methodist Episcopalian Church was opened in 1857. Renamed Albert College in 1866, it became a university with the power to grant degrees a year later. Since 1884 the Albert College has operated as a secondary school.

Emmanuel Episcopal Church

Holloway Street United Church

Fire destroyed most of the old buildings in 1917 and a new, magnificent Gothic stone structure was built in 1926.

Separate schools in Belleville had their beginnings in the 1830's. In 1882 a convent was erected on the site of the present St. Michael's High School and a select school for boys and girls was opened at the time.

On October 20, 1870, Lieutenant Governor Howland opened a provincial school for deaf children at Belleville with three registered students attending the ceremonies. Known today as *Sir James Whitney School,* it is one of the largest and best equipped institutes of its kind on the North American continent.

On March 13, 1970, the then Governor-General of Canada, Roland Michener, laid the cornerstone of the first permanent structure on the campus of Loyalist College, a community college established at Belleville in the 1960's.

The Methodists were the first to erect a church in Belleville in 1818. It was enlarged in 1831 and replaced in 1847 with a brick-veneer building. A stone edifice built in the 1860's was the first Methodist church in Upper Canada to have a spire on top of its tower and a bell to call the congregation. Fire destroyed this church in 1886 and a new church, the present Bridge Street United Church, was opened the following year.

The first St. Thomas Anglican Church in Belleville was in use by 1820. The frame building was replaced by an imposing stone structure in 1858. Destroyed by fire in 1876, the church was rebuilt on the same cornerstone three years later. In 1975 St. Thomas Anglican Church once again burned. Work to restore and rebuild the historic old church began at once. On November 7, 1976 the restored church was consecrated.

The history of St. Andrew's Presbyterian Church goes back to 1821, but it was not until 1831 that the congregation built their first church. In 1870 the frame structure was replaced by a brick building. Like most of the city's early churches, it, too, burned to the ground. In 1895 the present St. Andrew's Church was erected on the site of the former church.

St. John's Church

The present Tabernacle Church was built in 1877. Spires which for many years graced its two towers have long since been removed, but the church standing on the brow of a hill remains as one of the landmarks of the past.

The parish of St. Michael the Archangel had its beginnings in the early 1800's. Under Father Michael Brennan who came to Belleville in 1829, the first Roman Catholic church was built. A larger stone church was erected in 1837. When it, too, became inadequate for the growing congregation, a new church was built in the 1880's. This church was destroyed by fire on Christmas Eve, 1904. Although there was no insurance, rebuilding began immediately and the present church of St. Michael the Archangel was opened in 1905.

Bridge St. West Flood in 1918

The first library organized in 1876 was known as the Mechanics' Institute. It became the Belleville Free Library in 1902. In 1908 Senator and Mrs. Henry Corby of Belleville presented a building to the citizens of Belleville "for their sole and only use forever as a free public library". Along with this gift they set up a trust fund stipulating that the interest from it be used for the purchase of books.

"Glanmore", one of the city's remaining Victorian mansions, today houses the Hastings County Museum which has one of the finest collections of historical displays in Ontario.

A small weekly newspaper, the *Anglo-Canadian*, published in 1831, was the first of a number of short-lived papers to appear in Belleville. The *Weekly Intelligencer*, founded in 1834, became the ancestor of the present *Intelligencer*, one of the four oldest surviving newspapers in Ontario, having maintained continuous publication.

Canadian National Railway Station, Belleville

Built in 1838, the County Court House and Gaol stood for 122 years on the brow of a hill on Pinnacle Street in Belleville. A new County Administration Building was erected on the site in 1960.

The railway came to Belleville in the 1850's. On October 27, 1856, the first passenger train stopped at the Belleville Grand Trunk station on its initial Toronto-Montreal run. Soon after, Belleville was made a divisional point in the Grand Trunk system and the railway became one of its largest employers.

Thompson's Sash, Door, Shingle & Planing Factory

The lumber industry responsible for Belleville's earlier prosperity declined by the 1870's. The rich timber resources to the north of the city were exhausted. Sawmills and lumber manufacturing plants closed. Only after the turn of the century did Belleville resume its growth. During the 1920's a number of larger industries established plants in the city. Others followed in the thirties and forties. A large Industrial Park in the northeast end of the city, near the Macdonald-Cartier Freeway, today is the home of a growing number of diverse industries that are trading around the world.

Attractive parks, modern shopping centres, and highrise buildings are rapidly changing the face of the historic city on the Bay.

Dynamic and on the move, Belleville looks to a bright and happy future as its citizens pause to celebrate the 100th birthday of their progressive city.

This view of the Belleville harbour in the 1830's was sketched by Thomas Burrowes.

The large two-storey building on the east bank of the river was the Wallbridge residence which stood at the northeast corner of Front and Dundas Streets. The house built by Asa Yeomans was originally an inn operated by Margaret Simpson who, in 1798 with her husband John, had opened the first tavern in the settlement that was to become Belleville. The inn was sold in the 1820's to the Wallbridge family who converted it into an elegant residence. Sadly neglected in recent years, the house was Belleville's oldest surviving dwelling until the spring of 1973 when it was demolished.

The island in the centre of the sketch, long since connected by a causeway to the shore, is now part of Victoria Park.

The Belleville Harbour in the early 1830's

Thomas Burrowes sketched this view of the east hill of Belleville and the lower bridge across the Moira River in the early 1830's.

St. Michael's Roman Catholic Church can be seen in the upper left; St. Andrew's Presbyterian Church, a frame building at that time, is shown between the sign posts; and in the upper right is St. Thomas Anglican Church. The sign advertises an "Inn and Travellers' Rest" in the village. Buildings on the left near the river bank are mills.

View of Belleville in the early 1830's

This sketch of the Moira River and Coleman Street from the vicinity of the lower bridge by Thomas Burrowes, shows what appears to be the McNabb's flouring mill on the east bank of the river. This flouring mill and Meyers' sawmill were both situated at Meyers' dam just above two islands. On the west bank of the Moira is a cloth mill and farther upstream on the island Frost's sash and door factory.

Moira River and Coleman Street in the early 1830's

John Walden Meyers, United Empire Loyalist and founder of Belleville, constructed the first sawmill on the east bank of the Moira River around 1790. Soon after, he added a gristmill to which settlers came from as far away as Smith's Creek (Port Hope). The Captain's various business enterprises which eventually also included a distillery and a brick kiln helped to establish Belleville as a prosperous community. Until 1816 the settlement was called Meyers' Creek.

The remains of Captain Meyers' mill still stand on Station Street, a thoroughfare known in the early days as Mill Street.

Captain Meyers' Mill on Station Street

The Hastings County Court House and Gaol on the brow of the hill on Pinnacle Street in Belleville, were constructed in 1838 at the cost of $23,640. Thomas Rogers of Kingston was the architect.

In 1839 the first Quarter Sessions were held in the Court House with Benjamin Dougall presiding. Edmund Murney then was the Clerk of the Peace, and J.W.D. Moodie, husband of noted writer Susanna Moodie, the Sheriff.

In the foreground of the picture is the Merchants' Bank of Canada at the corner of Pinnacle and Campbell Streets. This building was later purchased by Senator and Mrs. Henry Corby who had it remodelled and presented it in 1908 to the City for a public library.

Court House and Merchants' Bank

A flour mill once operated a short distance north of Belleville on the Moira River. Known as the Moira Mill, it was owned by S. A. Lazier & Sons. Mr. Lazier, a descendant of one of the earliest settlers in the area, acquired the mill in 1872. Originally it was a paper mill with the flour business being added at a later date.

Lazier's Mills on Moira River, Belleville, Ont.

Lazier's Mill on the Moira River

The old Hastings County Court House built in 1838 stood on the Pinnacle Street hill for one hundred and twenty-two years and its courtroom was the scene of many a court battle fought by brilliant lawyers.

Four massive columns supporting the portico in front of the court house were fashioned from the trunks of trees believed to have come from the orchard of Captain Meyers, the man who is considered the founder of Belleville. The western slope of the hill was terraced and planted with trees, and for many years it was a favourite site on which celebrations of historic significance were staged.

In 1960 the Court House was demolished to make way for a new county administration building.

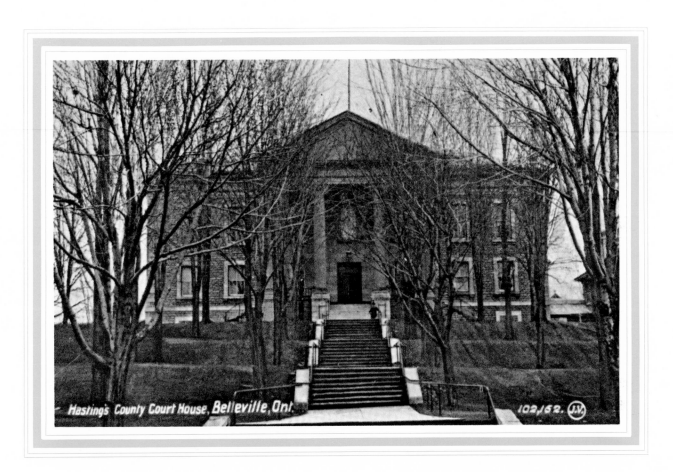

County Court House

Panter's Park is situated on the west bank of the Moira River, just south of the Lower Bridge in Belleville. It was named in honour of William H. Panter who was mayor of Belleville in 1915.

The park has been landscaped in recent years and in 1970 an astrolabe sundial and a commemorative plaque were installed at the site.

Panter's Park and Moira River

The original library building on Pinnacle and Campbell Streets was presented by Senator and Mrs. Henry Corby to the citizens of Belleville in 1908 "for their sole and only use forever as a free public library." Along with this gift a trust fund of $20,000 was set up, the interest from which was to be used for the purchase of books.

A library had been organized in Belleville in 1876 by the Mechanics' Institute. At the time it became the Belleville Free Library in 1902, library rooms are believed to have been located above a store at the corner of Front Street and Victoria Avenue.

The three-storey building on Pinnacle and Campbell Streets as it is shown in the picture was erected in the mid-1800's by the Merchants' Bank of Canada and housed the banking office and the residence of the bank's manager before it was purchased and remodelled by Senator Corby to serve as a library. The first major addition to the building was constructed in 1959. A new children's section was added in 1968, and in the fall of 1973 a two-storey extension known as the Delaney Wing in honour of Chief Librarian Olive Delaney was opened to the public.

Corby Public Library,
Belleville, Ont, Canada.

Corby Public Library

R everend Thomas Campbell, the first Rector of St. Thomas Church, supervised the building of the first house of worship at this site prior to 1820.

A second church, completed in 1858, then stood on the brow of this hill at Bridge and Church Streets until 1876, when it burned to the ground. The congregation rebuilt their church on the same cornerstone and St. Thomas once again opened for services on December 28, 1879.

Almost a hundred years later, on the morning of April 30, 1975, this historic old Belleville church shown in the picture, was destroyed by fire when thieves broke into the building. Only the outer walls and the tower remained standing, but rebuilding began at once and the restored house of worship was consecrated on November 7, 1976.

St. Thomas Anglican Church

The present Bridge Street United Church on the northwest corner of Church and Bridge Streets was dedicated on May 12, 1887, the dedication sermon being preached by the Reverend Dr. Potts from Toronto.

The church replaced an earlier house of worship on this site built in 1865 and destroyed by fire on January 6, 1886. It had been the first Methodist Church in Upper Canada to have a spire topping its tower and a bell calling its congregation to worship.

The congregation of what is now Bridge Street United Church goes back to 1815 when it was formally organized and plans were made to erect the first house of worship in the settlement. A rough frame structure was subsequently built in 1818 on the west side of Pinnacle Street (now the site of the Royal Canadian Legion building). This church was enlarged in 1831 and sixteen years later it was replaced with a brick-veneer building which remained in use as a church until the 1860's.

Billa Flint, one of Belleville's leading citizens, donated the lot at Church and Bridge Streets and here the cornerstone of a new church was laid on May 24, 1864.

Bridge Street United Church

Victoria Avenue Baptist Church on the corner of Pinnacle Street and Victoria Avenue was erected in 1907. The Baptists of Belleville built their first church in the 1870's at Coleman and Moira Streets. By the 1890's the congregation had outgrown the small structure and the property was exchanged for a lot and building at the present site. The building had been a roller skating rink before becoming the home of a business college and extensive remodelling was required to convert it into a place of worship. It served the congregation until the present edifice was constructed under the Reverend E. H. Emerson.

Baptist Church and Victoria Avenue, Belleville, Ont., Canada

Baptist Church, Victoria Avenue

The parish of the Church of St. Michael the Archangel on Church Street had its beginnings in the early 1800's. Under Father Michael Brennan, the first resident parish priest, a small wooden church was built on this site in 1829. It was replaced by a stone structure in 1837.

Construction of a new and larger edifice, similar in design to the present church, commenced in 1886. On Christmas Eve, 1904, the magnificent building burned to the ground. Although there was little insurance, the congregation under the Reverend Augustine Twomey began restoration at once and before the end of 1905 the present Church of St. Michael the Archangel had risen from the ashes.

Roman Catholic Church of St. Michael the Archangel

The present St. Andrew's Presbyterian Church with its stately spires and gables was built in 1895. It replaced an earlier brick structure which had been erected here at the southeast corner of Victoria Avenue and Church Street in 1870, and was destroyed by fire twenty-four years later.

The origin of St. Andrew's goes back to 1821 when the government granted one acre of land to a small congregation of the Church of Scotland. The first house of worship, a neat frame structure painted white, was erected at the site in 1831. The Reverend James Ketcham was the first minister of St. Andrew's.

St. Andrew's Presbyterian Church, Belleville, Ont., Canada

St. Andrew's Presbyterian Church

Christ Church at the corner of Coleman and Catherine Streets was first opened for services on Easter Sunday, 1882. A beautiful edifice of Gothic architecture, this Anglican church replaced an earlier structure which had stood on Moira Street and had burned to the ground on April 25, 1881.

One of the magnificent windows in the present church commemorates the Reverend Dr. W. C. Clarke, the Rector under whom the church was built.

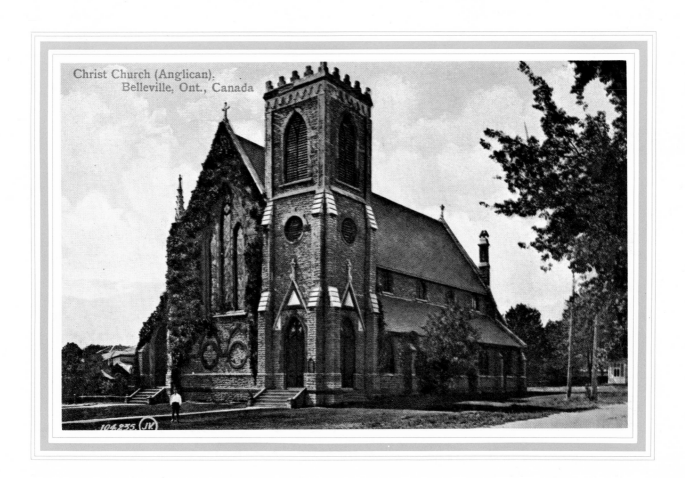

Christ Church, Anglican, Coleman Street

Belleville owes its first hospital to a group of public-spirited women. As a result of the efforts of Mrs. Harriet Jacques, wife of the Principal of Albert College, the Women's Christian Association came into being in 1879. On June 2, 1880, eighty members of the association obtained a charter which empowered them to build a hospital and a home for the needy.

Faced not only with financial problems, the women also had to put up with attacks by the press, the city council and people on the street who accused them of attracting the poor of the county to be supported by the city. Undaunted, the women laboured for five years selling homemade articles, holding rummage sales, giving speeches, and soliciting funds. On July 25, 1885, Mrs. Nathan Jones, the Association's inaugural President, turned the first sod at the present site of the hospital. A year later, on July 20th, the combined hospital and home for the aged was opened. The east wing was added in 1890 and in 1911 the south wing was completed. By 1948 the Belleville General Hospital had become too large an operation for the Women's Christian Association. It was given as an outright gift to the City of Belleville along with a government grant of $100,000. the women had received. A new complex of modern buildings has since replaced the old buildings on the south side of Dundas Street East.

City Hospital, Belleville, Ont., Canada

Belleville Hospital

Belleville City Hall on Front Street was built in 1872-73 by local contractor John Fortin.[x] One of the finest examples of Gothic architecture, the old landmark with its graceful tower has weathered more than a century.

The original design had called for a shorter, stubby tower but as work progressed Fortin[x] insisted that the square clock tower be raised to a height of 185 feet above street level. There are experts today who consider the Belleville City Hall tower better proportioned than the Peace Tower in Ottawa.

In December of 1873 workmen put the finishing touches on the building and installed the big tower clock, and a cast iron bell which had been imported from England. On Christmas Eve that year, Bellevillians gathered downtown to see the four clock faces in the tower lit up for the first time. Unfortunately, not enough gas jets had been installed and the dials that night were barely visible against the sky.

During 1874 the Town Council and the Police Court took up their quarters in the new municipal building. Eventually the market was transferred to the ground floor of City Hall where it remained until the mid-1900's.

x correction: Fotin

Belleville City Hall

The brick building at the Lower Bridge on the northeast corner of Bridge and Coleman Streets in this bird's-eye view of west Belleville of the early 1900's housed a "Livery, Hack, Sales and Stables" establishment. Across from it, at Coleman and Bridge Streets, was the Windsor Hotel. The building on the southeast corner of Bridge and Coleman Streets was occupied by the Belleville Marble Works. Christ Church on Coleman Street can be seen in the upper right. The church spire in the background appears to have belonged to Holloway Street Church.

Birds Eye View of West Belleville and Lower Bridge, Ont., Canada

Bird's-eye View of West Belleville

The Hotel Quinte on the northeast corner of Pinnacle and Bridge Streets was erected in 1895 on the site of the former Dafoe House, one of the city's oldest landmarks, which had been destroyed by fire nine years before.

The first manager of the hotel was Charles Hunter, formerly a clerk at the Dafoe House.

Hotel Quinte
Belleville, Ont.

Hotel Quinte

The Post Office at the corner of Bridge and Pinnacle Streets was a familiar landmark to Bellevillians from the late 1800's to the 1960's when the old building was demolished to make way for the new home of the *Intelligencer*, Belleville's newspaper founded in 1834.

There was a time when the mail had to be picked up at the post office by the recipient. It was not until 1913 that a letter carrier system went into effect in Belleville. On the morning of Saturday, May 24th of that year the letter carriers lined up in front of the post office to be photographed before starting out on their first routes.

The Post Office and Customs Office. Belleville, Ont., Canada

Post Office and Customs Office

This view shows to the left the Hotel Quinte, corner of Pinnacle and Bridge Streets. Behind the hotel is Bridge Street Methodist Church, now known as Bridge Street United Church. In the foreground, on the right, are the Armouries, and the building in the background is the Belleville Opera House. Later known as the Griffin Opera House, this substantial brick structure was erected in 1883 at the southwest corner of Bridge and Church Streets to replace an earlier Opera House at Pinnacle and Campbell Streets which had been destroyed by fire.

For years the Opera House was the centre of activities not only for Belleville but also for the surrounding area, and its walls resounded to the music of Carmen, or the hit tunes of the day. Lively vaudeville acts, dancing girls in gaudy costumes, local talent such as the Dumb Bells, artists of international renown, itinerant minstrels, jugglers and magicians enthralled the audiences. With the gradual encroachment of movies, particularly the "talkies", on live performances, the Opera House had to close its doors in the late 1920's and a few years later the historic old building was demolished.

Pinnacle and Bridge Streets, looking east

In the horse and buggy days the Belleville Market located on the square behind City Hall was one of the liveliest markets in Ontario.

The market building to the right was erected in 1850 as the first town hall and was used for public and entertainment purposes. At one time the ground floor housed the meat market where butchers kept their stalls. In 1905 the building was converted into the city police station. The police office and cells occupied the lower floor, while the upper storey was taken up by the police courtroom and the health office. The old building was demolished in the 1960's when the police department moved to the former Y.M.C.A. building on Campbell Street.

The Market, Belleville, Ont.

Belleville Market

A number of Belleville's magnificent old churches are located on this street, once shaded with many trees. To the left is Bridge Street United Church built in 1887 as a Methodist house of worship. On the hill opposite it stands St. Thomas Anglican Church, erected in 1879.

Church Street looking North,
Belleville, Ont., Canada

Church Street looking north

The House of Refuge was erected by the County of Hastings in the early 1900's on the north side of Dundas Street East just east of McDonald Avenue which in those days formed the city's eastern limits.

The first resident to be admitted to the Home in January 1908 was 80 year old Henry Sharp from Sidney Township. The building served as a home for the aged until 1951 when the new Hastings Manor was opened on Trent Road. Superintendent at that time was Ken Yorke.

The old House of Refuge was sold to private interests and stood vacant for the next quarter century. In the summer of 1977 the massive brick structure was finally demolished.

House of Refuge, Belleville, Ont.

House of Refuge, Dundas Street East

The Young Men's Christian Association first organized in Belleville around 1892, erected a building on Campbell Street in 1911. As the YMCA, by its own definition, was "interdenominational and for rich and poor alike", the building soon became the focal point of community life.

The building served the city as a meeting place and for a variety of programs of activities and services until 1964 when the YMCA moved into a modern new complex on Victoria Avenue. The Campbell Street building was taken over by the Belleville Police Department in 1965.

Y.M.C.A. Building, Campbell Street

In the foreground is the footbridge connecting a lane from Front Street with Coleman Street at Catherine. In the background is the Lower Bridge at Bridge Street.

The footbridge in the picture replaced an earlier structure swept away in the spring of 1918. On the morning of March 20th of that year the ice breaking up in the river had begun to shove down from the Upper Bridge and by noon it came to rest against the footbridge. The dam it formed caused the Moira to overflow and within a short time Front Street was under several feet of water. Before long the old footbridge gave way and was carried downstream piling into the Lower Bridge.

Bridges over Moira River, Belleville, Ont.

Bridges over the Moira River

Buildings on the east side of Front Street in the early 1900's included, starting in the foreground: The Standard Bank, Tom's Cafe, Howe and Hagerman's tin shop and store, Veterans Hall, Green's butcher shop, Molson's Bank, City Hall, Chamber of Commerce. On the west side of the street were located: Day's Pool Room, Black's Candy Shop, Royal Bank, Ed Thomas's store, Bishop Seeds and the Daily Ontario Steam Printing House.

Front Street looking south

Here at the "Four Corners" where Bridge Street crosses Front Street in downtown Belleville, was the home of the Merchants' Bank of Canada. In 1922 the Merchants' Bank merged with the Bank of Montreal, and a short time later the Bank of Montreal moved to this building from its former location at the southeast corner of Pinnacle Street and Victoria Avenue.

Bridge Street, Belleville, Ont., Canada

Bridge Street looking east

The buildings located on the south side of Bridge Street in the late 1800's, starting at the Pinnacle Street corner and going west are the Post Office; Pitceathly & Kelso's wholesale grocery warehouse; Wallbridge and Clark's liquor store and grocery; and the Standard Bank at the corner of Front Street. To the left is the City Hall tower.

The Post Office and Bridge Street, Belleville. Ont., Canada.

Bridge Street looking west

Front Street, Belleville's principal business thoroughfare, was not yet paved in the early 1900's.

On the east side of Front Street, near the Four corners at Bridge Street, was the location of O. S. Hicks' grocery store. Farther north at Campbell Street stands the Bank of Commerce building, and across from it, also on Campbell Street, was once the home of the Union Bank.

The upstairs of the building on the west side of Front Street across from Hicks' store was occupied at that time by the Ontario Business College, a school founded in the late 1860's, and attracting students from various parts of the world. Other business establishments on the west side of Front Street going north included, next to the Dominion Bank, Arthur McGee's tailor shop, Fish's men's furnishings, Simmons' furnishings, Sulman's fancy goods, Dunnit's dry goods, Cumming's harness shop, Spangenberg's jewellery store, Gough's men's wear, McFee's jewellery store, Haines and Lockett's shoe store, Conger Bros. grocery, Walker's hardware and Sam Retallack's men's wear store.

Front Street looking north

The Belleville Armouries on Bridge and Pinnacle Streets were built in 1907, replacing an earlier building on Church Street. The site on which the Armouries now stand was once the property of Dr. George Couper whose house, surrounded by beautiful gardens, faced on Pinnacle Street.

Over the years the Armouries have been the scene of many an important event connected with the city's proud military tradition.

The Armouries

The original Grand Trunk Railway Station on Station Street is now a part of the Canadian National Railway Station.

On October 27, 1856, the first passenger train steamed into the Grand Trunk depot at Belleville on its inaugural Toronto-Montreal run. Crowds lined the tracks long before the train was due to arrive, and the mayor of Belleville was on hand to greet the railway officials and dignitaries aboard the history-making train.

"Belleville has at last been placed upon the great highway . . . ", wrote the *Intelligencer* of the day.

G.T.R. Station, Belleville, Ont., Canada

Grand Trunk Railway Station

Now known as the *Sir James Whitney School* in honour of the former Premier of Ontario, this provincial school for deaf children is located on Dundas Street West in Belleville.

The school was opened as the "Ontario Institute for the Education of the Deaf and Dumb" on October 20, 1870 by Sir William Pearce Howland, then the Lieutenant-Governor of the Province. The first three registered students attended the opening ceremonies. Dr. J. W. Palmer was the first principal of the school.

The Ontario Institute for the Education of the Deaf and Dumb, Belleville, Ont., Canada

The Ontario School for the Deaf

The site of St. Michael's Academy at Church Street and Victoria Avenue was originally designated as a hospital lot and later was used as a ball park and parade ground. It was purchased by St. Michael's Roman Catholic Church and in 1907 the first school building was erected there under the Reverend D. A. Twomey. The school was destroyed by fire in 1929 leaving only the stone walls standing, but under the Reverend C. J. Killeen it was rebuilt the following year.

Since then St. Michael's Junior School adjacent to the academy has been opened and a former convent building at the site has become St. Michael's High School. To the north, on Church Street, Nicholson Catholic College named after a former pastor of the parish was completed in 1959.

St. Michael's Academy, Belleville, Ont., Canada

St. Michael's Academy

The cornerstone of the present Belleville Collegiate Institute and Vocational School on Church Street was laid on October 5, 1927 by the Hon. J. S. Martin who also officiated at the opening ceremonies of the school on December 12, 1928.

The new school replaced the former Belleville High School, a brick building which had stood on this site since 1874, having been the successor of the County Grammar School erected in the 1840's. Known as the Union School when it first opened its doors, the High School shared the premises with the Central Public School for a number of years before taking over the entire building.

At the close of the school term in the summer of 1927 workmen began to demolish the High School to make way for the new structure.

Now the oldest of Belleville's secondary schools. B.C.I.V.S. has spacious classrooms, two gymnasiums, a large cafeteria, and an auditorium which seats approximately one thousand people.

Collegiate, Technical and Vocational School, Belleville, Ont., Canada.

Belleville Collegiate

Albert College, a magnificent stone structure of traditional collegiate Gothic design was built in 1926. It is situated on the Trent Road surrounded by picturesque grounds and overlooking the Bay of Quinte and the rolling hills of Prince Edward County.

The College had its origin in the Belleville Seminary, a centre for higher Christian education founded by members of the Methodist Episcopalian Church in 1857. Renamed Albert College in 1866, it became a university with the power to grant degrees. Federated with Victoria College in 1884, Albert College then became a secondary school and since 1925 has been a part of the United Church of Canada. Students are coming from all parts of the world to attend the College.

The original college buildings were located on the north side of College Street, but were destroyed by fire in 1917.

Albert College

Billa Flint, a native of Brockville who took up residence in Belleville in 1829 and was to become one of the community's leading industrialists, erected the picturesque Tuscan-style villa at Bridge and Ann Streets in 1860.

In the early 1900's the house, surrounded by spacious grounds, was converted into a school for young ladies. Known as St. Agnes Manor, the rambling place then contained a number of apartments in recent years. The building was demolished in the spring of 1973 to make way for a modern highrise.

St. Agnes Manor

This old frame house on Dundas Street East, opposite the Belleville General Hospital, was the homestead of George Bleecker, a hardy pioneer farmer of Loyalist ancestry. He built the farmhouse at the rear in 1824 and some twenty years later, when he had prospered, he added two large reception rooms at the front.

The Bleeckers, George and Tobias, owned two hundred acres of land stretching from the Bay shore to present-day Station Street. Bleecker Avenue, named after these pioneers, was the western boundary of their property.

Bleecker House

Known as the Ponton house, this stone residence on Dundas Street West was built long before Belleville was a town, by William Hutton, grandfather of the late Colonel William Ponton.

Hutton, a well educated Irish farmer, came to Canada in the 1830's to seek a new home for his wife and family. He settled on the Bay of Quinte and first lived in a farmhouse which he had purchased with his property. Part of this farmhouse was later incorporated as the kitchen wing in Hutton's new home.

A square building with a hip roof and a wide verandah, the house once possessed all the characteristics of an English Regency cottage. As time went on the porches were removed and a small tower, popular in the Victorian era, was added.

Ponton House

Built in the 1830's the small stone cottage with the gable roof on Dundas Street East, between George and Ann Streets, once housed the general store of John Maybee. For many years it was a stopping place for weary travellers on the stagecoach route between Kingston and Toronto.

Today, the old landmark is a part of the Belleville Animal Hospital.

Belleville Animal Hospital

The charming stone cottage at Sinclair and Bridge Streets was once the home of John Weddeburne Dunbar Moodie, the first Sheriff of Hastings County. His wife, Susanna (Strickland) Moodie, has become famous in Canadian literature with her books *Roughing it in the Bush* and *Life in the Clearings,* both vivid accounts of pioneer life in Upper Canada based on her own experience. Susanna called the house her "haven of rest", and legend has it that on occasion her ghost still visits her old parlour.

The house was designed and built by George and Hannah Cooper around 1835.

Susanna Moodie House

This Scottish cottage on the Bay of Quinte, south of Highway 2 and opposite the Palmer Road, goes back to the area's pioneer days. It was built by Alexander Chisholm, a Loyalist and one of the first settlers in this part of Upper Canada.

A Scot by birth, Chisholm had first emigrated to Albany. During the American Revolution he went to Quebec to serve with the British. After the war he received a land grant on the Bay of Quinte in compensation for his services.

The story has been handed down that in 1812 General Isaac Brock on his way to York stopped and rested at the Chisholm home.

Alexander Chisholm House

David D. Bogart, a prosperous Belleville lumber merchant, built this residence resembling a chateau at the corner of East Bridge and John Streets in the mid-1800's. During that period the mansard roof was a popular feature, not only because it provided additional living space but also was a kind of status symbol.

One of the owners in the early part of the 20th century had the house painted in a striking shade of pink reminiscent of similar homes in southern France.

Bogard House

Glanmore, a stately Victorian mansion at the corner of Bridge Street East and Dufferin Avenue, now houses the Hastings County Museum.

A mixture of Second Empire and Italianate architectural styles, the house was designed by Montreal architect Thomas Heanley and was built in 1882 for Belleville banker John Philpot Curran Phillips. The interior, planned for the luxurious living of a well-to-do family and with much of its original grandeur preserved, features a sweeping main staircase, wall and ceiling frescoes, ornate furniture, carpets and draperies.

Because of its architecture, the spacious brick house with its bay windows and mansard roof decorated with cast iron cresting was declared an historic site of national importance in 1969.

Glanmore

This picture of the Belleville waterfront in the 1970's shows the rear view of buildings on the west side of Front Street opposite City Hall. To the left are the steeple of the Church of St. Michael the Archangel and the city's water tower.

Belleville Waterfront

The modern County Administration Building on Pinnacle Street was erected on the site of the old County Court House in 1960. Officially opened on January 18, 1961, the building is designed to combine under one roof the functions of justice, administration and registration formerly housed in three separate structures.

The court house portion of the new building is jointly owned by the County of Hastings, the City of Belleville and the Town of Trenton. The section which is occupied by the County Administrative Offices is the property of the county.

County Administration Building

Stores and business establishments on the east side of Front Street looking south in the early 1970's include the Singer Company, followed by a restaurant, Dover's men's wear store, Muntz Stereo Centre, McCoy's drugstore, the Family Bakery, McKnight's Variety store, a barber shop, the Cosy Grill Restaurant and the Bank of Montreal at the Four Corners. The buildings across Bridge Street once occupied by Tip Top Tailors, and the Paragon Café, have since been demolished to make way for the Century Place complex. Next to the café is the home of the Duke of Edinburgh Unit of the Army, Navy and Air Force Veterans (under renovation), followed by James Texts' bookstore, the Victoria & Grey Trust Company at the corner of McAnnany Street, and across from it the City Hall.

Front Street looking south

Century Place, a 5½ million dollar structure at the southeast corner of Front and Bridge Streets, was the brainchild of a number of local businessmen who envisaged the project as the beginning of a redevelopment of Belleville's downtown core.

The modern complex of shops and offices was designed by architect Eberhard Zeidler and constructed by Cornerstone Builders of Belleville. Demolition of twelve existing buildings commenced in January 1975 and excavation work on the first phase of the project began in April of that year. Just twelve months later on April 1, 1976, two anchor tenants, Bell Canada and Guaranty Trust, moved into the premises, followed soon after by a variety of shops and tenants occupying office space in the building. Phase Two of the development slated to be carried out at a later date will be co-ordinated with the construction of a parking garage and other new commercial ventures.

At the Century Place site once stood the home of the Standard Bank, an imposing building at the Four Corners occupied in more recent years by Tip Top Tailors.

Century Place

Picture Credits

Albert College, 133

Anderson, Allen, 75, 77, 97, 113, 117, 121, 125

Belleville City Hall, 53

Canadian National Railways, 60

Century Place, 157

Corby Public Library, 71

Dempsey, W. A., 54

Hastings County Museum, 16, 28, 32, 34, 35

Historical Atlas, Hastings County, 8, 22, 23, 36

Intelligencer, 24

Mika Collections, 15, 69, 73, 79, 81, 83, 85, 87, 89, 91, 93, 95,
99, 101, 103, 105, 107, 109, 111, 115, 119,
123, 127, 129, 131, 135, 137, 139, 141, 143,
145, 147, 149, 151, 153, 155

Public Archives of Ontario, Toronto, 63, 65, 67

Pages 5 to 7, and 11 to 52, have been reprinted from the *Daily Intelligencer*, courtesy of *The Intelligencer*, Belleville, Ontario.

H6

COURT HOUSE &